THE BLACKAPINO

THE BLACKAPINO

Michael Goodloe

Copyright © Michael Goodloe

All rights reserved.

Published by Blackapino Press

ISBN-13: 979-8-9938668-2-6

This book is dedicated first and foremost to my children, who may one day find themselves wondering about the man their father truly is. May this narrative offer them clarity, connection, and a deeper understanding of my purpose, struggles, and triumphs, illuminating the ways my journey has shaped their own.

It's also dedicated to those, like me, navigating life between races, cultures, and identities—your story echoes here, too.

PREFACE

I've been called "ambiguous," "exotic," even "hard to place."

But I'm not a mystery—I'm a mix.

Black and Filipino. Brown-skinned in a world that still measures worth in proximity to whiteness.

In some spaces, I'm "not Filipino enough." In others, I'm "not Black enough."

And yet, I carry both lineages like rhythm in my blood—the food, the slang, the silence, the grief.

The truth is, I'm not half of anything.

I'm whole, just not what most people expect when they hear the label.

A cultural theorist once wrote about the borderlands—those in-between spaces where people live at the edges of identity, forging new ways of being out of contradiction. That idea speaks directly to my life. I've spent most of my time at the intersection of multiple worlds: Black and Filipino, traditional and contemporary, American but not quite mainstream. I've existed in rooms where I was too Black for some, not Black enough for others. Too Asian for one crowd, unrecognizably Asian for another. I've felt the pressure to code-switch, to explain myself, to make others comfortable with the version of me they could understand.

But with time, I've come to see that racial ambiguity is not a limitation—it's a lens. A perspective shaped by complexity, layered experiences, and the ability to move between spaces that rarely speak to each other. I've learned how to be *both/and* rather than *either/or*. And while that hasn't always been easy, it's given me a way to see the world that's deeply rooted in empathy, adaptability, and truth.

This memoir is not just about identity. It's about the places and people that shaped me—family, loss, relationships, work, and the ever-shifting terrain of race in America. It's about navigating boardrooms and barbershops, grief and love, misunderstandings and small victories. It's about what it means to belong everywhere and nowhere at once—and to still find a way forward.

By telling my story, I hope to offer others who live in the in-between a sense of recognition. We don't always get a clear lane. But we learn how to make one. And sometimes, standing at the crossroads gives you the best view of all.

WHERE ARE YOU FROM

I don't believe in stupid questions.

I do, however, believe people often ask the wrong questions—searching for an answer they can't quite articulate. Like a girlfriend dissecting the plot points of my day without ever asking how my day actually went.

The same thing happens in social interactions. People are drawn to mystery. Not just beauty. Not just physical features that make you do a double take—but something deeper. An energy. An aura. A frequency that makes people curious before they even realize why. Some might call it a higher vibration.

I feel it all the time. But the moment I acknowledge it, I shut the thought down. I've never wanted to be the guy who walks into a room assuming he's the hottest thing in town.

Still, I've always been aware of my surroundings—the details, the shifts in body language, the unspoken tension between people who haven't yet decided if they should introduce themselves. And eventually, as my presence becomes harder to ignore, I do what I've always done: create an opening.

I make myself approachable. I soften the edges of an interaction before it even begins. After the pandemic, social skills became a lost art. And icebreakers? Even worse. Dating apps had to *force* people into conversation starters. And yet somehow, people still fumble the most basic interactions in person.

Which brings me to the inevitable question:

"Where are you from?"

I know what you really mean.

You're not asking where I grew up. You're trying to place me. Trying to decode what your eyes can't quite figure out.

It's funny—there's an unspoken rule that you don't outright ask a man about his ethnicity. It's considered taboo. But I can always tell when that's the real question sitting on the tip of someone's tongue. Whether you're a beautiful woman or a random guy standing next to me, the icebreaker will almost always be:

"So, where are you from?"

And with a smile on my face, I always respond:

"I'm from here."

The confusion and smirk usually come first. Then the follow-up, their eyes narrowing as they try to place me. And inevitably:

"I mean . . . what are you?"

It happens so often I can almost predict the tone before they say it. Some are hesitant. Others direct. A few are bold enough to skip the "where" and go straight to "what." And every time, I wonder: *Are they asking because they're genuinely curious? Because they feel entitled to an answer? Or because my presence—my ambiguity—disrupts something they thought they understood?*

This question follows me throughout my life: at interviews, meetings, networking events—even at casual social gatherings.

I remember one fall afternoon, early in the season. I was shopping for a shirt at one of my favorite stores—Zara. This was before Zara got "woke" with their men's line. Back when their idea of fashion-forward didn't always include space for someone like me.

Since my build is skinny but not short, I've always preferred Zara's European cuts and how their slim-fit button-ups complement my frame. I usually shop at the Westfield Mall location in Montgomery County, Maryland—they tend to carry more casual wear than other spots, and I could always hit the food court right after.

On this particular day, I was prepping for a night out with some friends. We had a table reserved at our favorite spot, Lux Lounge—the latest hip-hop club in DC. Lux had a strict dress code for men, but it was worth it. Some of the most stylish, urban socialites in the city parlayed there regularly, and I was happy to indulge.

As I browsed the racks for something new, I noticed a beautiful Ethiopian—or maybe Eritrean—girl working the floor. She caught my eye immediately. She didn't approach right away, but she greeted me with a bright smile and lingered nearby as I looked through the latest drops. I eventually landed on a gray dress shirt with a silk-blend texture and subtle black leopard print. It had a smooth, elevated feel to it—something that fit my natural sense of style. Confident in my pick, I took it to the counter.

She met me at the register. Before I could say anything, she asked with a warm smile: "Did you find what you were looking for?"

"Yeah," I answered quickly, trying to keep it cool.

She seemed bubbly and lighthearted, flashing another smile as she removed the tags. Maybe it was my fresh haircut or the fact that I'd actually put some thought into my casual outfit. I've always been told—*look your best, even if you're just running errands. You never know who you'll meet.*

As I watched her work, she looked up and politely asked: "Can I ask you a personal question?"

Now my antennas were up. *What could she possibly want to know about me?*

She leaned in slightly. "Where are you from?"

I gave her my best half-smile and said, "I'm from Laurel."

She didn't miss a beat. "What about your mom?"

Oh, I thought. *You're really curious about me.*

So, I opened up a little. "My mom's Filipino. My dad's Black."

The reaction was immediate—like she'd just won a surprise blind date with the amazing voice behind the curtain. She lit up and told me I looked very handsome, that my unique appearance made me stand out.

It's always been difficult for me to accept compliments from beautiful women. Sometimes, I don't feel worthy of them. My blend of two worlds—worlds that often feel like they're defined by separation—has been a blessing, but it's also a journey. One, I've had to learn how to carry with grace.

The phrase *"Where are you from?"* was rarely just small talk—it carried a weight that felt anything but innocent. I heard it from all angles, often wrapped in a tone that made it clear: this wasn't curiosity, it was a challenge. A subtle way to signal that something about me didn't quite sit right with them—like they were trying to solve a puzzle they didn't think I had the right to be part of. At times, it felt like a sneak diss—meant to poke at a part of me they assumed was unsettled, unsure.

Looking back, I see now that many of these moments were micro aggressions, camouflaged as conversation. Passive-aggressive power plays, especially from men who felt threatened in rooms where attention was being shared. Social settings could bring that out—another man might try to expose or mock my ambiguity, hoping to lower me in the eyes of others, especially women. For some, it worked—especially the ones who made it a joke. That's partly why I never liked nicknames or teasing as a form of bonding. I always preferred calling people by their names. Maybe it was my quiet way of preserving dignity in others and myself.

I tread carefully when speaking about other races, especially when it comes to how I've been treated. These conversations can get messy, but the truth is—everyone holds onto stereotypes, whether they admit it or not. We all carry some inherited assumptions, shaped by the world around us. When I hear *"Where are you from?"* from both Black folks and white folks, the tone doesn't always differ much. Sometimes it's lighthearted—genuinely curious, even if a bit clumsy. Other times, it comes from a more narcissistic place, as if my existence is just a performance for their amusement. In those moments, I'm not a person—I'm a curiosity, a spectacle. Someone to be labeled, prodded, or dismissed as just another "mut" fishing for attention.

REFLECTIONS ON IDENTITY

My ethnic background is Black and Filipino. My father is 100% Black American, and my mother is Filipino. Now, I'm pretty sure my mom's side has its mix—somewhere in there, her dad may have had Chinese ancestry, and her mom was likely of Asian and Spanish descent. I once dug into that rabbit hole, trying to understand the full scope of my Filipino heritage.

But truthfully? I'm not ready to 23-and-Me my life away.

So I've made peace with the mystery. Even though there's a disconnect on my mom's side, I embrace what I do know.

The thing about being Black and Filipino is—people rarely guess it right. Some see my skin tone and assume I'm just Black. Others notice something in my features and guess Latino or Pacific Islander. And then some don't even bother guessing—they just ask:

"What are you?"

Like I'm a riddle they *need* to solve.

The thing is, those answers are never just about facts. They reveal what people expect. What categories they're comfortable with. And depending on where I am, the answer I give can change the way I'm treated—before I even open my mouth.

An honest opinion I hold is that Filipino people are like the Mexicans of Asian society. A comedian once said that, and I have to admit—I knew exactly what he meant. Filipinos are known for their hard work, resilience, and tight-knit communities—values that remind me of my mother's experience immigrating to the US. Like many first-generation Filipino immigrants, she worked restaurant jobs without complaint. For her, making it to America wasn't just about surviving—it was about building something better for the next generation.

I remember being in fifth grade when a Mexican girl in my class asked about my ethnicity. When I told her I was Filipino, she gave me this pompous look and dropped an unsolicited fact: Spain invaded the Philippines and enslaved our people for 333 years. Even though the comment stung, it was true—and that moment stuck with me.

There are so many microaggressions directed at Filipinos, often rooted in the idea that *Asian-American* identity primarily centers around East Asians. Look at how Chinese, Japanese, and Korean communities are portrayed—socialized as intelligent, wealthy, and perched at the top of the Asian hierarchy. In contrast, Filipinos and Vietnamese are often seen as outsiders: intellectually inferior, working-class, and even prone to crime.

Filipinos, in many ways, are treated as the *other* Asians—just as

Mexicans are sometimes viewed within the Latino world. Maybe that's why I've always felt like an anomaly—too Black to be fully embraced as Asian, too Asian to be fully understood as Black.

My father's lineage is deeply rooted in Black American history. If my mother represents *movement*—the immigrant journey—then my father's family represents *foundation*, though no less complex. According to a family tree my uncle put together, our ties to Africa feel distant. My Blackness has always been something I've understood through an American lens.

What's interesting about my ethnic duality is that not only am I not white—I also carry the weight of two second-class identities. It's like the odds were already stacked against me, and now I had to decide which part of myself I was allowed to express more. It's like being forced to pick a racial identity for your driver's license: Black, Asian, or *Other*?

I hated the idea of playing both sides of the fence—but this was my reality. My record. My identity.

> *"A double-minded man is unstable in all his ways."*
> James 1:8

And maybe the answer was already there.

I identified as Black.

LIFE IN THE BORDERLANDS

I was raised on the East Coast, in Laurel, Maryland. The state of Maryland sits uniquely positioned as a border state due to the historical controversy over the Mason-Dixon line—a symbolic boundary that still echoes past tensions between North and South. It's as if I were born right into the heart of America's historical drama. Today, this region is commonly recognized as the DMV—a collective acronym for DC, Maryland, and Virginia.

At its center is Washington, D.C., the nation's capital, famously known as "Chocolate City" due to its historically large Black community and vibrant African American culture. Nowadays, DC has become a magnet for ambitious transplants eager to pursue careers in politics, technology, or simply to reinvent themselves. The city pulses with a diverse energy, defined by its blend of monumental architecture, bustling streets, and the constant hum of political ambition.

MICHAEL GOODLOE

Across the Potomac River lies Virginia, affectionately and bluntly known among my friends and many native DMV locals as a place you "don't fuck around and find out." Northern Virginia historically skewed predominantly Caucasian, with communities characterized by manicured suburbs, affluent schools, and a proximity to government and defense industry jobs. Venturing further south into rural Virginia often meant encountering areas still quietly marked by histories of racial division, places that could quickly become uncomfortable for Black and Brown people traveling alone. Yet, in recent decades, Northern Virginia has also transformed, welcoming large immigrant communities, notably from East Africa, adding vibrant cultural layers to previously homogeneous neighborhoods.

Maryland, however, carried its own distinct identity—often misunderstood by outsiders as synonymous solely with Baltimore. While Baltimore proudly boasts delicious crab cakes, rich history, and gritty charm—and despite my nearly decade-long stint working in Baltimore City—it irritated me whenever outsiders defaulted to assuming all Marylanders hailed from there.

Unlike New Yorkers, who identified through boroughs, or Atlantans who connected through wards, Maryland residents clarified their identities through their specific cities and towns. Laurel was uniquely situated, serving as a crossroads town nestled between major cultural hubs—positioned neatly halfway between Baltimore and DC. This town occupied a fascinating middle-ground, neither fully suburban nor entirely urban, embodying influences from both major cities. An intriguing quirk of Laurel was its geographic placement—within just a twelve-mile radius, it intersected four separate counties. The particular part of Laurel you called home had a significant influence on your lived experience.

My family settled in South Laurel, located in Prince George's County, the county known for its vibrant Black communities, but also recognized as having a tougher reputation compared to surrounding areas. Life there offered its own blend of community strength and urban struggle. The demographic encompassed all areas if you rated their household income and family size. The part of Laurel I was raised in was distinctly black-centric compared to West Laurel or Laurel proper, which visibly carried the signs of generational wealth through well-manicured lawns and spacious homes. Our side, conversely, was marked by layers of apartment complexes, where families like mine sought stability, not luxury. It was here, amid the close-knit clusters of apartments and townhomes, that many young families began laying their foundations, sending their children off to one of the many elementary and middle schools tucked within these neighborhoods. Eventually, our disparate paths would converge at Laurel High School.

I always valued our community's intimacy, not just because it was familiar, but because it offered tangible opportunities to grow through work and hustle. Between my brother and me, we held positions up and down Route 1, where life buzzed around restaurants, shops, and small businesses. The proximity fostered independence and ambition, but it also subtly underscored the limits placed on us—limits set not by ambition but by perception.

Being situated on the PG County side of Laurel meant confronting an added, uncomfortable reality: policing seemed less about protection and more about surveillance and suspicion. Nights that should've been uneventful walks home became tense exercises in survival. Frequently, just the act of walking while Black prompted unwanted interactions with undercover officers or patrolling vehicles, each encounter chipping away at our sense of belonging. I vividly remember one night, my friend and I had barely crossed the street from his building when two undercover officers abruptly confronted us, guns drawn, claiming we matched some vague description. What description exactly? It seemed to boil down simply to being Black, wearing coats in the chill of the night. The moment was jarring and left an indelible mark of vulnerability.

Even mundane tasks became charged with suspicion. One afternoon, while simply washing my BMW—a car that symbolized personal achievement but also made me a target—I was abruptly questioned by a white officer who demanded my license and insurance. To him, a young black man comfortably handling a luxury vehicle was an anomaly, worthy of interrogation. Such encounters felt like cruel pranks played repeatedly, a relentless reminder of where society believed I belonged.

Before cellphones could document encounters and social media lawyers could offer instantaneous advice, I relied on wisdom from my elders. Their instructions—remain calm, be respectful, comply—echoed in my ears during these tense moments. Despite my racial ambiguity elsewhere, to law enforcement, I was always unmistakably Black, always in the wrong place at the wrong time.

This stark contrast in policing did not exist in other parts of Laurel, areas shielded by privilege and a different demographic makeup. The fear of being harassed in your own neighborhood was a unique burden to the South Side, the perceived "bad" side of any American town. Within South Laurel, we had four notable neighborhoods: Kimberly Gardens, Town Center, Pumpkin Hill, and my own, Fox Rest. Each neighborhood had its crews, tight-knit groups of friends who established identity and respect among peers. Our group was known as FRC—the Fox Rest Crew. It was more than camaraderie; it was our face card, our social currency, our way of asserting worth and belonging in a place where external judgments often threatened our sense of self. I will attest that in comparison to the greater part of PG County, it wasn't as harsh as areas like Suitland, Landover, or Capitol Heights. If you ever catch the Showtime documentary of Kevin Durant, *Basketball County: In the Water*, he goes into greater detail, illustrating the nuances of life in various parts of the county and underscoring the relative privilege, albeit limited, we experienced in Laurel.

Growing up in the DMV, I navigated this assorted cultural tapestry constantly. Even within this rich diversity, my racial identity remained complicated. Being both Black and Filipino often left me uncategorized or miscategorized. Too light-skinned to neatly fit into typical Black stereotypes, yet too culturally distinct to blend fully with my Asian peers, I found myself frequently labeled "not Black enough" or "not Asian enough." Each neighborhood, each school, each friendship group brought its own set of nuanced expectations, making my experience a perpetual balancing act between multiple worlds.

But the DMV—despite its contradictions—fast taught me code-switching and adaptability. The mix of military families, government workers, and immigrant households meant I was constantly around different accents, customs, and expectations. You had to learn how to move between spaces quickly.

One moment I'd be chopping it up with my Black friends about the latest mixtape, and the next I'd be walking into a Filipino household where everyone called me *anak* and handed me a plate of pancit and lumpia before I even sat down.

That duality—belonging everywhere but never quite fitting in—shaped the way I moved through the world.

GROWING UP

Where I come from, you couldn't afford to be ignorant about your surroundings. Especially the people you kept around you. Folks were straightforward—sometimes brutally honest. But they could still be on some bullshit. I was constantly asked as a kid, "What are you?" and I quickly realized—I wasn't like everyone else.

It's wild to think I'm in my late thirties now, knocking on the door of forty. If you saw me, you probably wouldn't peg me as a father of three, let alone someone inching toward Unc status.

I was born in 1987, the younger brother to Aaron—my late brother—who was just a year older than me. We were raised in Maryland, military kids, but without the constant relocation. My father had already settled into the best part of his Navy career, working as a cryptologist for the NSA. That was a big deal, considering where he came from—Gary, Indiana.

A city known for three things: being the murder capital, the birthplace of Michael Jackson, and the backdrop of one of my favorite Black films—*Original Gangstas*.

My mother, on the other hand, spent her life in the food service industry. Before she met my father, she had been married once and had two sons. As I mentioned earlier, that part of her life remains a mystery to me. Maybe it was easier that way.

What I do know is that my parents' story is almost cliche—military man meets beautiful foreign woman. My father was the definition of a strong Black man: commanding, sometimes aggressive, and not always expressive with his love. My mother, being Filipino, had a different way of showing affection, which probably made me a mama's boy by default.

She adored my brother and me—maybe even more so because we were born with Cooley's anemia, a rare blood disorder linked to both our African and Asian heritage. It made her extra protective, always ensuring we were safe, cared for, and maybe even a little sheltered.

Growing up, I felt the constant push and pull of these two identities—my father's world of discipline and survival, my mother's world of tenderness and tradition. And right in the middle of it all was me, living in the in-between. Not fully one thing. Not fully another. Just . . . me.

Maybe this sounds narcissistic, but I believe being a millennial baby, combined with the uniqueness of my racial identity, sets me apart. Sometimes I sit back and reflect on how far I've come—how I navigated the chaos and cultural shifts of society without completely losing my mind.

The '90s were a wild time to grow up, especially for two half-Black, half-Filipino kids surrounded by straight-up, no-doubt-about-it Black folks. And I mean that in the best way. The joy of growing up in the '90s feels unmatched compared to the way kids experience life today.

Even the way I raise my own children doesn't come close to the freedom I had back then. It's wild to think about—how much time we spent outside, how little supervision there was. We didn't have multiple TVs in the house, and definitely not in our rooms. If I wanted to play Nintendo, it wasn't just a press of a button. I had to earn it.

I'd plead with my dad to let me hook it up to the one TV in the living room—which, of course, he had already claimed for himself. If I lost that battle, I was out the door, looking for the next best way to entertain myself.

A lot of my days were spent outside—climbing trees, playing in the dirt, finding adventure in the smallest things. I'd sit and watch ants pile into a molehill, fascinated by how they moved in sync, never breaking rhythm. At night, fireflies lit up the dark like tiny floating lanterns, and I'd chase them around the yard, trying to cup their glow in my hands.

We had bikes, too. My brother—always ahead of me—would be zooming up and down the street while I was still stuck on training wheels, wobbling behind him, trying to keep up.

One of the best things about our apartment was that it was on the ground floor with a walkout patio. That sliding glass door was *the* entrance. Nobody ever knocked on our front door. It was like an unspoken rule.

Friends, cousins, even random neighborhood kids who somehow became part of the crew—they all knew to walk up to the patio.

Someone was either already outside, chilling, or just on the other side of the glass, ready to slide it open.

As I got older, the streetlights became our unofficial curfew. We could roam the neighborhood all day—no phone, no check-ins—just the understanding that once those amber lights buzzed on, it was time to head back.

Our favorite spot was this little convenience store called the *Video Stop*. While other kids might have had Blockbuster nights with their families, we had *Video Stop*, run by a Korean lady who seemed to have everything—from the latest VHS rentals to every snack a kid could want. That place was a ritual for us.

There *was* a 7-Eleven in the neighborhood for a while, but it didn't last. It got robbed too many times and eventually shut down. But *Video Stop*? That was different. It was small, but it had a soul.

My dad would take us there to rent movies, and that was his ritual, too—but for different reasons. He had this whole bootlegging system worked out. He'd dub the tapes so we could rewatch them without having to rent them again, stacking up a collection of grainy VHS copies labeled in his handwriting.

Looking back, that was my introduction to hustling in its own way—figuring out how to stretch a dollar, how to make things last longer than they were supposed to.

Those years were simple, but they shaped me. There was no Wi-Fi, no endless stream of entertainment at our fingertips. We made do with what we had, and somehow, that felt like more.

THE BLACKAPINO

Most of my childhood, we had someone extra living with us—an uncle, a cousin, or a friend—stacked in our two-bedroom, one-bath apartment. One year, my Uncle Joe lived with us, and to me, he was the coolest guy in the world.

He wasn't just some relative crashing on our couch—he was like a big brother. Someone who actually saw us. He made us feel like we weren't just kids, but his little proteges.

Uncle Joe had that early '90s swagger—rocking a fresh Bobby Brown cut and moving through the world like a real-life Casanova. He played basketball, had a smooth way of talking, and man, the girls he pulled? *Next level.*

I'll never forget the day he brought this one girl over. She was fine—light-skinned, long, curly hair, like a real-life Tisha Campbell from *House Party*. That was his movie, by the way. He put my brother and me on to it, and looking back, I think he was low-key trying to live that life.

I watched how he talked to her, how he made her laugh without even trying—and I knew right then: my uncle had game. And I wanted to be like that.

But for all his charm, Uncle Joe didn't last long in my dad's house. His cool points couldn't save him when it came to discipline, and my dad wasn't the type to play around.

Joe kept getting in trouble—skipping school, letting people into the house when my parents weren't home, treating the place like it was his own bachelor pad.

The final straw? My dad caught him messing with his vinyl records, trying to DJ on a turntable like he knew what he was doing. That didn't go over well. Not in my dad's house.

The one family member from my dad's side who actually stuck around for the long haul was my Uncle Willy. And when I say he was Black, I mean *Black Black*—from the way he talked, to the way he dressed, to the way he moved through the world. There was nothing watered down about Uncle Willy.

He had that don't-mess-with-me energy—the kind of presence that made people take him seriously without him having to say much.

Before he came to live with us, I remember getting letters from him. Looking back, I'm pretty sure he was in jail at the time. He never said it outright, but the letters had this weight to them—like he was writing from a place he didn't want to be.

Still, he never made it dark. He'd always include a superhero drawing on a separate page—something for me and my brother to look forward to. I held on to those drawings like they were treasures.

Unlike Uncle Joe, Uncle Willy wasn't blood-related. He was from New York but had moved to Indiana as a kid, where he met my dad. They grew up together, practically brothers, and my dad took him in when he needed a place to land.

He was the fun uncle—the one who would let you sneak a sip of his beer or stay up late watching *Friday the 13th* when he babysat. He put my brother and me on to all the classics—*Ninja Turtles*, *Ghostbusters*, *Nightmare on Elm Street*. If it was dope, Uncle Willy knew about it first.

But what I loved most about him was the way he made everything feel *real*. He didn't talk to us like little kids—he talked to us like we were equals.

If something was wack, he'd tell us straight up. If we were acting soft, he'd toughen us up. And if he grilled some BBQ, you *knew* it

THE BLACKAPINO

was about to be the best meal of your life.

Uncle Joe was cool, but he was a phase. Uncle Willy? He was family.

We were living that '90s middle-class package of bougie-ghetto—not quite struggling, but not quite balling either.

Black culture was everywhere in our home, shaping me more than anything. Nights were filled with 2Pac blasting or whatever old-school vinyl my pops decided to throw on. I can remember nights of Con Funk Shun playing for hours. Endless Prince songs mixed with Michael Jackson.

My favorite moments were when he'd put *The Box* on, and we'd watch 2Pac music videos. He bought every 2Pac album, and I knew every verse. It was like Jesus speaking to me—the messages, the beats, they made me feel passionate about what he was saying.

My dad was the definition of an OG at the time—Newport in one hand, a glass of cognac in the other, drowning the house in music.

The '90s were a golden era for Black entertainment—sitcoms were booming, hip-hop was shifting culture, and every weekend, my dad and his military crew were throwing house parties like it was their job.

What was funny, though, was how almost all of my dad's military friends had Filipino wives—except for one, who married a white woman. Most of them were Black, but there were a couple of white guys around, too. I don't know what was in the water, but everybody was drinking it. These parties were always lit—Black men with stable, well-paying government jobs, married to Filipina women who held it down for them. And most of them had kids around my age. That's when I started noticing—I was cut from a different cloth.

Take my cousin, for example. She could pass as 100% Black if she wanted to—deep cocoa complexion, thick curly hair. Her sister was lighter, more caramel, but still undeniably Black. Then there was my older male cousin, who looked like me and my brother—lighter skin, straight hair—but something about him felt more Filipino. Even though he carried himself like a smooth Black dude, his facial features leaned more Asian. That was the thing about being mixed—people read you differently depending on who was looking.

But growing up around all this diversity, I never thought twice about why my dad and his boys fell for Filipinas. It was just the norm. My cousin Josh, though—he always had jokes about his stepmom and the rest of the Filipino women. There was something about the dialect that made it easy to poke fun at, and we could find humor in almost every conversation. We'd get fussed at in Tagalog, and even that was funny to us.

By the way, my cousin Josh was the stepson to my aunt—she married a man who already had three kids, all 100% Black: Josh, Sean, and Hope. That made five of them total when you included Randa and Nina, the Blasian sisters. They were my tribe—I spent endless days and nights at their house, sometimes because my dad was too inebriated to drive us home. We'd just crash there, and by morning, we'd wake up and do it all over again like it was an unspoken routine. I spent most of my time with Miranda and Josh—Miranda because we were close in age, and Josh because he was the middle child, too young to run with Big Sean and Hope, but old enough to vibe with us.

One of my favorite memories was sitting around the kids' dinner table, unknowingly absorbing Filipino culture in ways that would stick with me forever. It wasn't something we thought about back then—it was just how things were. We ate almost every meal with our hands, scooping up rice and meat like it was second nature. Utensils weren't really a thing unless we were serving food onto our plates. It wasn't until later in life that we realized how much of our habits were tied to our Filipino side, passed down in the simplest, most natural ways.

Looking back, I realize I was surrounded by shades of Blackness, by layers of identity that blended and overlapped in ways I didn't fully understand at the time. But even then, I knew I was different—I just didn't have the words for it. There were always reminders—like when Miranda's extended family came by, or when friends who had never seen me before showed up. The first question was always the same: *Whose kids are these?* It wasn't asked in a mean-spirited way, more out of curiosity—like they were trying to piece together a puzzle that didn't quite fit.

The aunties, in particular, never failed to comment on our looks, always marveling at our good hair and the unique mix of our facial features. *So handsome!* they'd say, as if our appearance alone made us special.

At the time, I didn't think much of it. It was just something that happened, something I got used to. But looking back, I realize it was one of the earliest signs that I existed in this in-between space—not quite one thing, not quite the other, but intriguing enough for people to take notice.

It's a shared experience I now know many mixed kids had—something social media has given a name to. Thanks to Instagram handles like Justin LaBoy, I see now this wasn't just *my* experience—it was a whole thing. A weird, unspoken rite of passage for kids who grew up not looking exactly like either side of their family, yet somehow embodying both.

It wasn't until I hit eleven or twelve that I started feeling like my identity wasn't entirely mine to define. Up until then, I had never questioned where I fit in—I had a Black dad, Black cousins, and even Blasian cousins. But by middle school, things shifted. Suddenly, people weren't just interested in *who* I was; they were more focused on *what* I was.

Middle school is its own battlefield. Seventh and eighth graders don't sugarcoat anything, and I was constantly fielding questions about my race. It wasn't just the unsolicited *"What are you?"*—it was the unsolicited opinions that came with it. I went to a pretty balanced school with a mix of Black and white kids, plus a handful of others. But when you're racially ambiguous in a place like that, you're constantly being sorted—whether you like it or not.

Growing up, my best friend was Trent, and he was white. We had been tight since elementary school and stuck together all the way up to eleventh grade—until he got expelled for stealing a guy's car. He played baseball, so naturally, I ended up hanging out with other white kids from his team. We were inseparable—everybody knew we were locked in. But at the same time, I had my brother, and *he* had a best friend who was Black. They saw me drifting into this mostly white social circle, and that's when the teasing started.

Apparently, I was starting to "sound white."

I had no idea what that even meant at the time, but the jokes were relentless. They were just jokes—at least that's how they were delivered—but deep down, it made me wonder: Was I doing something wrong? Was I supposed to sound a certain way?

It wasn't just about how I talked—it was the whole image people were crafting around me. I started noticing how different I felt depending on who I was around. With my white friends, I was "exotic" enough to be interesting but never "too Black" to make them uncomfortable. At school, I was *the Blasian kid with the white voice.* I hung out mostly with white kids, had a white best friend, and even dated the hottest white girl in my class. That made me "cool" in one crowd but suspect in another. And just like that, I cemented my popularity with the white kids at school. When another one of my friend's white baseball teammates transferred in, that sealed it—I had officially become the token Black guy of my friend group.

I didn't resist it. If anything, I leaned into it—without realizing I was setting myself up for a long, complicated relationship with my own racial identity. I was evolving into *something,* but I had no clue what. I just knew that wherever I went—at home, at school, with my Black cousins, or with my white friends—I was always being *seen through* something. Through expectations. Through assumptions. Through whatever version of me made the most sense to the people around me.

My connection with Trent ran deep. We met in first grade and stayed close for the next eleven years, sharing the same schools and, in many ways, the same growing pains. Those years were exciting, unpredictable, and formative. My parents weren't travelers—they weren't even the type to go out much—so I experienced much of the world outside my home through Trent and his grandparents. He lived with them because his mother wasn't in a place to raise him, and even as a kid, I could feel the weight of that absence. I saw the resentment he carried toward her—quiet but sharp, like a wound that never quite closed.

From the outside, his life looked ideal to me. He had his own room, a collection of action figures, played sports, and most of all, he was consistent. He showed up. He was generous with his time, quick with a joke, and reliable in a way that felt rare. As we grew up, we learned a lot side by side—our first crushes, fallouts with friends, the strange transition from being kids to being expected to act like adults. In high school, those expectations sharpened. Trent became the social connector, the guy everyone looked to for a good time. His basement became *the* hangout spot—complete with a side door and a privacy gate, like a secret clubhouse for teenage strategy. If something needed organizing, I was often the point of contact—his quiet copilot behind the scenes.

But over time, things shifted. Trent started doing things that sat uncomfortably with me. He had a need to control situations, to be right, to dominate—even when it wasn't called for. His charm could be manipulative, and that same charisma that made him magnetic could just as easily blur ethical lines. He'd stretch the truth to get what he wanted—whether it was money from his grandparents for a "school activity" that turned out to be a liquor run, or stories he spun to justify his next pursuit. He had a reputation for going after any girl he found attractive, and that energy followed him—people noticed. I started to see a pattern, and it made me think back to the way he treated his grandparents: tantrums, guilt trips, little performances to bend their will. It was like watching someone run a playbook they didn't even know they'd memorized.

Even with all his missteps, I remained Trent's best friend. My loyalty to him ran deep, partly because I had seen what he was capable of when someone crossed him—how quickly he could throw someone under the bus to protect himself. But he never did that to me. Not once. Maybe it was because I never gave him a reason to, or maybe he genuinely respected our bond. I saw firsthand the chaos he could spark—like during our senior week in Ocean City, Maryland. He was flirting with another guy's girlfriend, and by the end of the night, his car was keyed in retaliation. Trent didn't let it go. He grabbed a baseball bat and shattered the windows of the guy's '80s Camaro. The next morning, the police knocked on our door asking about the weapon. He could've kept quiet—they never found the bat—but to my surprise, he stepped up and took responsibility so none of us would go down for him. It was one of the few moments where he seemed aware of the weight of his actions.

But those moments of clarity were rare. His destructive behavior eventually caught up with him, cutting short what had once looked like a promising baseball career. His team was headed to Nationals in Florida, expected to win the whole thing. What I never told my friends was that their coach—and Zach's father—came to my house to ask if I would travel with the team. They believed I could keep the group grounded. I wasn't like the rest of them, and they knew it. I carried a moral compass that they lacked. I was the boundary.

Their instincts proved right: Trent got kicked out of the tournament for stealing alcohol from a grocery store.

That single moment changed everything. Zach and I were left to reevaluate the company we kept. I had to ask myself: do I stay loyal to someone who's spiraling, or do I invest in the kind of friendship that honors the history and values I live by? In the end, Zach and I moved forward without Trent. The memories stayed, but the friendship didn't.

My relationship with Zach had a different beginning than Trent. I didn't really get to know Zach until he started staying the night on the same weekends I was at Trent's house. Before that, it was like a separation of church and state—different lanes, different energies. But over time, our worlds started overlapping, and something about Zach's energy felt easy. He was more laid-back like me, but carried that effortless confidence—the kind that made him the life of the party without ever needing to announce it.

We agreed on most things and never disrespected one another. Maybe that's what made our friendship different from so many others: it wasn't built on competition, but on quiet understanding. We both came from homes where our parents cared, corrected, and instilled values. Zach had split time between two households after his parents separated, but instead of breaking him, it gave him perspective. He learned to adapt—to read the emotional temperature of a room—and I think that's what allowed us to connect.

What stood out most about Zach was his humility. He had access, resources, and a large family network, but he never flaunted it. There was an awareness to him, a kind of emotional intelligence that let him move through spaces with grace. In our early twenties, we spent countless nights out—beach trips, house parties, weekends that blurred into inside jokes and stories we'd retell for years. When most of our friends went off to college, we stayed behind and built our own kind of education—one rooted in people, places, and experience.

Looking back, I realize how much of my identity was being shaped in those years. Through Zach, I was invited into spaces that, on the surface, represented a kind of privilege I didn't grow up with. But instead of feeling out of place, I treated those moments like lessons. I watched how people moved, listened to how they talked about success, about family, about leisure—things I was still learning how to define for myself. I was studying culture, class, and confidence all at once, just by existing in those rooms.

At the same time, I'd bring Zach into my world—cookouts, game nights, block parties—where the rhythm was louder, the laughter longer, and the sense of family came without a filter. He fit right in, because authenticity doesn't have a race. It was almost poetic how easily we could cross each other's lines—me in spaces that reminded me how much I stood out, him in spaces where he was the only white face in the room—and neither of us had to perform to belong.

Maybe that's why I value Zach the way I do. He represented something rare: a friendship that existed beyond the surface. We met each other somewhere in the middle—between privilege and perspective, between Black and white, between comfort and curiosity. And maybe that's what true connection really is: not just finding people who understand where you come from, but who respect what you've had to navigate to get there.

In hindsight, I realize that my role in that group was never just about friendship—it was about balance. I was the one they called on when things might get out of hand, the one expected to de-escalate, to keep things "in check." At the time, I took it as a compliment—a sign of trust and respect. But with age, I've come to see the weight of that expectation. Being the moral compass wasn't just about character; it was racialized. I was the "safe one," the one who wouldn't cause trouble, the one who could blend in and calm the storm without making too many waves.

In a group of white guys, that perception gave me access, but it also came with pressure: to be more responsible, more level-headed, more careful—not just for me, but for them, too. It's a strange kind of invisibility, being counted on while also being quietly used. I didn't get to be reckless or messy without consequence. Trent could self-destruct and still have room to rebuild. I couldn't afford that luxury. And maybe that's why I outgrew it all before they even knew it was time to grow up.

That role—being the steady one, the grounded one—bled into how I navigated all spaces, not just with my friends, but with anyone trying to make sense of who I was. It wasn't just about managing behavior; it became about managing perception. And even though I was accepted by my white friends, I was never allowed to forget that I was different. Their trust didn't shield me from the constant reminders that I didn't fully belong. The questions didn't stop just because I was in the room. In fact, sometimes, being in the room meant I had to answer even more of them.

Even though I mostly hung out with my white friends, the social pressure around my racial identity never disappeared. Kids asked me all the time, *"What are you?"*—a question that wasn't just about curiosity but came loaded with judgment. And when I told the guys I was half Black, it was often met with disbelief. *"Yo daddy ain't Black."*

It was like my identity had to be seen to be believed—and since they never saw my dad, my word wasn't enough.

But when a girl asked?

That was different. I'd say I was half Filipino, and suddenly, I was interesting. Maybe it was the novelty, the mystery—either way, their reactions made me aware of how I could *shape* people's perceptions of me. It became second nature to emphasize my Blackness around guys and my Filipino side around girls. Looking back, I wonder—was that survival? Was I just adapting to what people wanted to hear? Or was I subtly trying to assert control in different spaces?

I don't know if I thought about it that deeply at the time, but I definitely felt like I had to play the game.

Interestingly, my white friends never saw the complexity of my identity at all. To them, I was just Black. They knew I was mixed, but they didn't care. Race wasn't something we talked about at thirteen—we were just kids trying to hang out.

But I always wondered—did their parents ask about me? And if they did, was their answer based on what I looked like?

By high school, the game changed. The bubble of middle school popped, and suddenly, I was in a real mixing bowl of people. This time, I wasn't just navigating friendships—I was navigating *where* I fit in. The upperclassmen had their own cliques, and for the first time, I met other multiracial people. It was a weird feeling. On the one hand, it was exciting to meet kids like me. On the other hand, I started realizing I wasn't as unique as I'd once thought.

Some seniors already knew what I was before I even said it. To them, a Black and Filipino kid wasn't rare—it was familiar.

But as I started branching out, things got complicated. My white best friend was still around, but our lives were diverging. He was deep into baseball, and our friend groups started shifting. And for the first time, I noticed something:

I wasn't getting the same attention from white girls anymore.

Middle school me—the "cool mixed kid"—had been intriguing. But high school was different. White girls gravitated toward white guys, and suddenly, I wasn't part of their world in the same way.

High school dating—or the lack of it—was complicated for me. I only had one real girlfriend, and that relationship lasted just a few months. It wasn't that I didn't *want* to date—it was that I was afraid. Afraid of rejection. Afraid of judgment. Afraid of what it would say about me, depending on who I pursued.

Looking back, I realize my racial identity played a huge role in that fear. It wasn't just the usual nerves of asking someone out. It was the silent, unspoken dynamic of attraction and race—the feeling that the girls I liked might hesitate because I wasn't what they were used to. I could feel it. It was almost like my ambiguity made things more complicated for them.

What's interesting is that, for three out of my four years in high school, I shared a locker row with two girls—one Trinidadian from New York, the other Jamaican. We talked all the time, and there was an ease in our conversations. Maybe it was because they were foreign, too—there was something about being around people who weren't just "American" that made things flow better.

But attraction? That wasn't there.

I don't know why. Maybe it was because they felt more like home—like friends, not potential girlfriends.

Then there was Maria. She wasn't one of my official locker mates, but she may as well have been. She was in my classes and basically claimed my locker because it was in a convenient spot. Lisa was Spanish—beautiful, with pale skin and these striking grey eyes.

I always felt like there was something between us, something unspoken that we never explored.

But I held back.

Maybe she did, too.

I don't know for sure, but every time we ran into each other at the lockers, she always had a Latin girlfriend with her. And I couldn't help but wonder—*was that my lane?* If I had put myself out there more, would Spanish girls have been into me? Was there an unspoken attraction I just never tapped into? Or was I overthinking everything, too caught up in my own insecurities to see what was right in front of me?

It's funny—I wasn't the type to go after every girl I found attractive, but I did notice who gravitated toward me. And more often than not, it wasn't white girls. By high school, they just weren't checking for me like that anymore. I had spent middle school being "popular with the Caucasian community," but in high school, that shifted.

I wasn't sure if it was because I wasn't white enough . . . or still too different to fully fit into their world.

And then there's the question of what *I* was drawn to. I liked browner skin, but I also found Maria's light complexion attractive. Was that preference—or was it social conditioning? Had growing up around certain beauty standards affected what I thought I liked? Even now, I wonder—was my hesitation more about them… or about me?

All I know is, when it came to dating in high school, I was always in my head. I had different friend groups, I got along with almost everybody—but when it came to actually making a move? I froze. Maybe it was fear of rejection. Or maybe it was fear of being accepted by the wrong person.

Either way, I let high school pass without really exploring what could've been.

At the same time, I started spending more time with my neighborhood friends—most of them Black, from places like Virginia, New York, and DC. Hanging with them, I gathered something else: how I spoke *mattered*. I wasn't just one of the guys right away—I had to prove I belonged. Slang, mannerisms, even the way I carried myself—it was all under a microscope in ways it hadn't been before.

By tenth grade, I realized I wasn't just one thing. I had different friend groups, different versions of myself depending on the room I was in.

But what I didn't know yet was *which version of me was really me.*

Uncle Joe, Aaron and me.

PEER PRESSURE

Those days at Fox Rest Apartments were some of the most memorable times of my life.

And it makes me wonder—do kids even go outside and just hang out anymore?

My own children don't, and we've moved three times in the last six years.

Back then, being outside was all we knew. There were no smartphones, no social media to keep us locked in. The neighborhood was our whole world. And I knew a lot of people, mostly through my older brother, who was just a year ahead of me in school. He had that natural charisma—the kind of social ease that let him bounce between different groups.

I, on the other hand, was more reserved—shy around people I didn't know well. But for the most part, we ran with the same crew. We had our day-one circle, the kids who had grown up with us. But then my brother introduced me to a new guy—Chris, from

New York.

Chris was different. He had that city energy—fast-talking, confident, always up to something. We had an on-and-off friendship because, in my opinion, he was always into some shit. And I wasn't trying to get caught up in the nonsense. The guys he gravitated toward were usually the misfits—the ones who got a kick out of breaking rules and stirring things up just to see what would happen.

One time, Chris convinced me to steal a trick bike that was left in front of the school over the weekend. Not just any bike—a GT, metallic blue with flake, four pegs, and gold-spoke rims.

It was the kind of bike that made you *somebody* in the neighborhood.

We rode that thing like we owned it. But karma always finds its way back.

Later that week, we stopped by Video Stop for snacks, and a group of guys from Town Center—a neighboring apartment complex—rolled up on us. One of them pointed at the bike.

"That's my bike."

Chris, always the instigator, hyped me up.

"Man, don't back down. Fuck them. They don't own the bike." I could feel the tension rising. I wasn't scared, but I wasn't stupid either.

Before things could escalate, Chris's uncle walked in. He was built like Suge Knight—tall as hell, light-skinned, bald head, thick beard. The kind of presence that made people move out the way. Just like that, the moment passed. We left the bike behind. Some things weren't worth the fight.

Chris had a way of pushing boundaries.

He wasn't just aggressive in what he did—he was aggressive in how he *spoke*. He was the one who really got me started on saying the word *nigga*. It's not like I hadn't heard it before—my dad and Uncle Willy used it all the time, mostly in a joking way. But I also knew there was a dark side to that word.

I'd seen it in movies, used with venom. I'd heard my mom weaponize it during fights with my dad—only she'd make sure to say it with the hard *-er* to twist the knife.

Chris, though? He used *nigga* like it was a comma—a constant in his vocabulary. One day, he asked me, "Why don't you say it?" I didn't have an answer. It wasn't that I never said it—I just didn't use it casually.

But peer pressure has a funny way of working. One day, I was hanging out with a group of guys I didn't normally kick it with, and I slipped the word into conversation. Everything stopped. The room went quiet. They looked at me—*really* looked at me. Then one of the older guys smirked and said, "You ain't no nigga."

It was half a joke, half a test. Before I could even respond, Chris jumped in. "Nah, fuck outta here. His daddy Black. What the fuck you talkin' about?" That ended the argument.

But it left me thinking.

It wasn't just about using a word—it was about *belonging*.

About proving something. I started to realize that aggression—whether in how you spoke, how you moved, or even how you carried yourself—was often seen as a measure of Blackness.

Being mixed was exhausting in ways I couldn't even explain back then. I was already teased for "sounding white," and now I was being called out for trying to sound too Black. It was a balancing act I never quite mastered. How you talked, the slang you used, even who you used it around—it all mattered. The rules were unspoken but strict. And the tricky part was, they changed depending on who was in the room.

I learned young that you had to read the room. Some Black kids saw guys like me—half-Black, mostly raised around Black people, but lighter-skinned, ethnically mixed—as Oreo niggas. Black on the outside, white on the inside. The ones who didn't say *nigga*, who mostly had white friends, who looked up to white role models. I wasn't that. But I wasn't fully part of the other side, either.

My influences were Black culture. It was the '90s—I wanted to be smooth like Denzel, funny like Eddie Murphy. I was already deep into Hip-Hop—2Pac, N.W.A., the R&B my dad and his friends blasted. My celebrity crushes? Adina Howard, Aaliyah, J. Lo, Halle Berry—any woman who graced the pages of *Black Men Magazine*.

And yet, even with all that, I still didn't always fit. There was always this underlying pressure—who was I supposed to be? Which parts of me were real, and which parts were just performance?

Once I graduated high school, all of that was left behind. The teasing, the questioning, the labels. It was up to me to define who I was.

And that was a journey in itself.

One day, I was coming home from work and noticed a car parked in my favorite spot. A light grey Grand Marquis with metallic flake, sitting on 22 inch rims. It was there all week, like it belonged more than I did. Eventually, I saw the guy who owned it—a tall, dark-skinned dude hanging out in front of the building, moving with that effortless confidence like he had already figured out the world.

Turns out, he had just moved in with his older brother. He was

Jamaican, five years older than me, and deep in his prime—an alpha male in full stride, living life on his terms as a migrant from Jamaica raised just outside of DC. From that first conversation, we clicked. I was fascinated by the way he psychoanalyzed people—his friends, women, even strangers. To him, human interaction was a sport. Every move was calculated, every situation had a deeper meaning. And no one was off-limits from his sharp humor—including me. He joked about me being Filipino all the time, but in a way that felt more like camaraderie than ridicule. Maybe because, in his eyes, I wasn't just another African American. There was common ground in being other.

The more time I spent with him, the more his world became mine. His family and friends became my family and friends. It was a completely different orbit, and I started moving within it naturally. But spending so much time with a crew of twenty-six— and twenty-seven-year-old men at seventeen had its consequences. I didn't see it at the time, but it changed the way people viewed me—especially my peers. They couldn't understand why I wasn't just hanging with people my age. I didn't even fully understand it myself. All I knew was that they saw something in me. They encouraged me to be myself, to own my look, my vibe. They used to joke that my brother and I were The B2K kids because of how we dressed and styled our hair—half a compliment, half a reminder that I stood out. But by then, I had heard every joke imaginable about being mixed.

What I did know was that being around them gave me a sense of power. Not just in how I carried myself, but in how others perceived me. We frequented all the local spots, and when I ran into old classmates or acquaintances, I wasn't alone—I was rolling with a crew of tall, well-dressed Jamaican guys who commanded attention. They had presence. A type of quiet authority that made people watch them when they walked into a room. And as a guy, that's a tool you don't take for granted—dressing the part, walking with confidence, speaking with intent.

This was the phase where I was experimenting—not just with my identity, but with a certain street persona. I learned the talk, perfected the look, and even started doing things I probably shouldn't have been doing. By the time I turned eighteen, I had moved to Pennsylvania to study advanced automotive technology. Cars had always been my thing, and I was the first one in my crew to get my license. I was tired of bumming rides. I wanted freedom—to move how I wanted, go where I wanted, and not have to wait on anyone.

My first car was a '91 Nissan Maxima, black-on-black with a Bose stereo. It was technically the old family car, but my parents had run it into the ground. To me, though, it was everything. I called it The Battle Max. That car took me places I probably shouldn't have gone, but it also made me feel untouchable.

Somewhere between dropping out of trade school and running the streets, I got involved with selling weed. It wasn't planned. It wasn't even on my radar. But I made a connection—a guy with some next-level exotic strains that no one else in the area had. Suddenly, I was the plug, the one with access. I wasn't just another dude trying to make ends meet. I had something people wanted, and with that came a certain power.

What's funny is, the person who got me into it wasn't even Black. It was my Korean friend, who was rooming with a couple of white guys who grew the Devil's Lettuce. The whole situation felt surreal. Here I was, a mixed kid raised in a Black household, being introduced to the drug game by an Asian guy in a house full of white dudes growing top-shelf weed. If there was ever proof that life doesn't follow a script, this was it.

But that was just the entry point. As time went on, I fell deeper into the streets, and this time, it wasn't with my old crew—it was with my Caribbean compadres. Something was intoxicating about the whole lifestyle. Fast money. Luxury cars. The sense of belonging that came with it. For the first time, I felt like I had control over my own narrative. I wasn't college-bound, I didn't come from wealth, and no one in my circle was showing me a different way.

So I followed the paper trail.

If you've ever listened to 50 Cent's *The Body Snatchers* mixtape, there's an interlude referencing *The Wire*—how, when you chase the money, you never know where it's gonna take you. That's exactly how it felt. I wasn't just playing a role anymore—I was living it. And the deeper I got, the harder it became to see another way.

Looking back, I realize I wasn't just searching for money, status, or even respect. I was searching for identity—for a place where I fit. I had spent years trying to balance my Black and Filipino sides, figuring out how I was supposed to move through different spaces. But here, in this world, there were no questions. No one cared how I talked or what percentage of my blood was Black. Either you could handle yourself, or you couldn't. Either you belonged, or you didn't.

And for the first time, I felt like I did.

That winter, I relocated to Gary, Indiana, to live with my aunt and uncle. At the time, I didn't fully grasp how much that move would shift my perspective—not just on life, but on myself. I had always been adaptable, able to blend into different worlds, but Gary was different. It wasn't just a change of scenery; it was a change of pace.

For the first time in a long time, I spent most of my days alone. My daily routine was a grind—an hour-long commute to school, another thirty minutes to my job, then back home to repeat the cycle. There were no familiar faces waiting for me after class, no crew to run the streets with. I had to learn how to be by myself in a way I never had before. At first, it felt like isolation. But over time, I started to embrace it. I found a kind of freedom in solitude.

Without the influence of my usual circles, I moved however I wanted. I'd drive around the city, deliberately getting lost just to see where the roads would take me. I'd eat dinner alone at random restaurants, not caring if I looked out of place. I even snuck into a hookah lounge using a fake ID, just to test the limits of this new independence. For the first time, I wasn't being pulled in any direction—I was moving on my own terms. No peer pressure, no expectations. Just me figuring out what I actually liked without anyone else's input.

But solitude has a way of being temporary, especially when you stand out.

At school, I quickly gained recognition—not just because I was one of the few Black students in a predominantly white automotive program, but because I was good at it. I excelled, and that put eyes on me. It was something I was used to—always being the anomaly in one way or another.

Then came the moment that would shift things again. A group of Filipino guys approached me one day, their expressions a mix of curiosity and familiarity. "Yo, are you Filipino?" one of them asked.

It wasn't the first time I'd been questioned about my identity, but this time was different. These weren't just people pointing out my mixed background; they were seeing it as a connection, not a contradiction. They had questions—where I was from, how Filipino I really was—but nothing about their tone felt doubtful or dismissive. It wasn't a test. It was recognition.

Meeting them was like stumbling into a room where I was already expected. For the first time, I wasn't just passing through different cultures, trying to fit in—I was invited in. They took me in like I was a lost brother, bringing me into their homes, sharing meals, and making space for me at their lunch tables. On weekends, we'd hang out, trading stories and experiences. It was a sigh of relief—a part of my identity that had always been distant was suddenly real, tangible, something I could actively participate in instead of just claiming.

One thing that stood out immediately was their sense of style. They were on point—rocking the freshest Jordans, but pairing them with Ralph Lauren shirts instead of the oversized white tees I was used to seeing in my old crew. It was a subtle difference, but a meaningful one. They had a polished, effortless swag—almost preppy streetwear before Kanye West made it mainstream. It was a small detail, but it made me think about how culture, even within the same racial or ethnic group, had layers.

That year in Gary gave me something I hadn't even realized I was looking for: validation. Not from the outside world, but from within myself. My racial ambiguity was no longer a weakness or something that made me feel othered—it was becoming a strength. Every time I found a new space where I was accepted, I realized that I wasn't half of anything. I was both.

When I eventually returned home, I saw things differently. The need to prove myself—to lean into one side or the other—wasn't as heavy anymore. Almost immediately, I reconnected with my Korean guy I introduced earlier. Before, I might have hesitated to dive into yet another cultural space. But now? Now, I was ready to explore every part of who I was, without feeling like I had to choose.

Gary, Indiana, might not have been where I expected to find clarity. But sometimes, stepping away from everything you know is the only way to truly see yourself.

Before I left for Indiana, JK and I had already built a tight bond while living in Pennsylvania. We had originally met through a mutual friend, but from the jump, it was like we had known each other for years. It was that instant chemistry—like a Dominic Toretto and Brian O'Conner situation from *Fast & Furious*. Two guys from different worlds, moving through life at full speed, drawn together by a mutual understanding.

At the time, I was still trying to carve out my own lane, but the reality was my attempts at independence hadn't exactly panned out. That's what led me to the Midwest. JK, on the other hand, was thriving. He was already deep in the car game—not just as a hobby, but as a lifestyle. His family had money—they owned a successful business—and that gave him the means to move differently. He was the first person I met who really had access to that world: high-end fashion, imported colognes, finely tuned sports cars. A modified RX-7, a tricked-out Evolution 8, a damn Matrix phone before anyone else had one. I was still making ends meet, pushing through life however I could. He had the blueprint; I was still drafting my plans.

What stood out about JK, though, was that he wasn't boxed in. Unlike the stereotype I'd subconsciously built about Koreans from a distance, he wasn't exclusive in who he surrounded himself with. He had white friends, Black friends, Caribbean friends, Filipino friends—he navigated different cultures the way I'd always tried to, effortlessly slipping between worlds. Maybe that's why we clicked.

In a way, he closed the loop on my Asian experience, even though he wasn't Filipino. He was the first to break things down in a way that made me think differently about race, identity, and the unspoken codes that came with them.

"You gotta move a certain way," he once told me. "Be more Asian and less Black."

I knew exactly what he meant.

It wasn't about rejecting one side of myself. It was about understanding perception—how people saw me, how they would categorize me before I even opened my mouth. Hanging around his circle, I was thrown headfirst into Chinese and Korean life. We'd watch their TV shows, eat at their restaurants, and celebrate birthdays and milestones while they spoke in Chinese or Korean around me. I wasn't just observing—I was inside their world, feeling the rhythm of their culture.

One thing I understood immediately: Asians stuck together. It wasn't just about pride or heritage—it was about strategy. They'd figured out a long time ago that unity was power, especially economically. Their families pooled money together, built businesses, created opportunities that kept wealth circulating within their communities. It was structured, intentional. And in many ways, it made me reflect on my own upbringing—the lack of generational wealth, the absence of that kind of built-in support system.

JK was blunt about it. "Most Asian women? You gotta impress them. And that usually means money or status."

It made sense. Everything around him reflected that ideology. His whole aesthetic was high-end—Louis Vuitton, YSL cologne, Hugo Boss jeans, designer watches. The way he carried himself, the way he spent money, the way he knew exactly how to move in spaces that valued status. Meanwhile, I was out here just trying to make my own way. I knew deep down that attracting an Asian woman—at least one who moved in those same circles—just wasn't in the cards for me at the time.

But it wasn't about women. It was about access.

Being around JK showed me that to fully assimilate into one side, you had to go all in or not at all. It wasn't enough to just "be" Asian. You had to live it, breathe it, embrace the cultural expectations that came with it. But I never wanted to be absorbed into just one world. That wasn't who I was.

I just wanted to be me—to move between cultures freely without constantly feeling like I had to prove something. To be accepted without conditions. To exist without the pressure of choosing a side.

Maybe that was my real struggle all along.

Because at the end of the day, I wasn't just navigating identity.

I was navigating inclusion.

Now that I had these different friend groups in my life, I felt like a reconstructed version of myself—like I had unlocked a multiverse of identities. Each version of me fit seamlessly into a different world, yet none of them defined me completely. I truly enjoyed the relationships I had built. If I wanted to embrace my Asian side, I had friends who welcomed me into their culture. If I wanted to party with my white friends, I could slip into that scene effortlessly. And when I needed to strip it all away, to just be me without performance, I could retreat to the comfort of my brother and our day-one crew from around the way.

But balancing it all? That was the real challenge.

It became a juggling act—one that took more out of me than I initially realized. Splitting my time between all these different circles felt like an endless game of shape-shifting. No matter where I was, someone always had something to say.

"Oh, you 'bout to go hang with the white boys over ya niggas?"

"Damn, you leaving us to chill with Ancient Chinese Secret?"

At first, I brushed it off as friendly banter, but after a while, it started to get to me. What had I become? Was I trying too hard to belong everywhere? Had I turned into a culture vulture, bouncing between groups like an outsider looking for a home?

Or was this just the cost of being racially ambiguous—never fully belonging to any one tribe, but always being expected to pick a side?

Maybe I was a victim of my own success, someone who'd spent years perfecting the art of inclusion only to realize that true belonging isn't about how many doors you can walk through—it's about feeling at home once you step inside.

But if there was one thing I knew, it was that peer pressure wasn't going to break me. It was only going to reveal a diamond.

Because in the end, I wasn't going to be bullied out of my own identity—not by pride, not by prejudice, not by anyone's expectations but my own.

THE SILENCES THAT SHAPED ME

My mother didn't talk much about feelings.

Not because she didn't have any—but because that wasn't how love worked in her world. In her Filipino upbringing, love was shown through duty, food, protection, and sacrifice. Words were too fragile. They could be misheard, misused, or misplaced. So, the important things were tucked into silence.

She didn't say, "I love you" often. But I never doubted it. I saw it in the way she packed my lunch with care, remembered how I liked pancakes for breakfast, and always made sure my brother and I were properly dressed every day. She worked the food hall at Fort Meade and came home exhausted, but still managed to cook pancit on birthdays and make sure the house was clean enough to keep her dignity.

That was her love language: consistency.

I reminisce on moments when my mom—or even my aunts—slaved at home to clean, cook, and listen to our whining. My mother and her sisters existed in the borderlands as an interracial couple. They had accepted a hybrid version of a traditional family, where the man worked and took care of the finances, and they were expected to raise the children and make a house a home. And yet they still worked full-time jobs. It was the cornerstone of the Filipino spirit—hardworking migrants whose resilience could not be removed.

But with that love came limits. We didn't talk about our emotions. Not deeply. If I had a bad day at school, she'd tell me to eat. If I seemed sad, she'd hand me the remote and let me choose what to watch. Comfort was offered, not explained. Vulnerability made her uneasy. Pain had to be swallowed and processed quietly—the way she had done when she left the Philippines at eighteen to start over in America.

As an adult, I get these flashbacks of arguments I overheard as a child. It was traumatizing at times to hear the abusive language that would fly back and forth between my parents. I would question why my mom allowed this verbal assault all these years, but as time went on, I came to accept that maybe that's just how normal marriages looked—at least in the world she came from. I kept waiting for a breakout moment, some scene where she would finally speak up and shut it all down with a snappy comeback. But it never came. It was like wishing on a falling star that never fell.

That's when I started to understand the limitations embedded in Asian culture as a whole. A silence of acceptance and submission. It played a theme throughout my life. I found myself shutting down during confrontations or disagreements. A part of me wanted to crash out and burn, but the trauma I'd absorbed from those feuds made me avoid back-and-forths altogether. But that wasn't always the case. Like most young adults, I indulged in partying, drinking, and reckless behavior. A drunk man tells no lies, and sometimes I would find my dad's spirit come to life through me—loud, belligerent, unfiltered. My friends from the neighborhood called it "Tupac Back." I had a sharp tongue—not just arguing, but cutting into people's character. I could get under the skin with precision. Then the morning after would come, and I'd sit with my guilt, replaying what I said and wondering if that was who I am.

This was the collision of Filipino masculinity and Black masculinity—emotional expectations I never consciously adopted, but that would flare up like anxiety attacks. One moment I'm the reserved, soft spoken, quiet guy and the next I'm the aggressive black guy. I wouldn't call it being bipolar, but when you're young and dumb, the filter is gone. I get subtle reminders of that phase every time Facebook shows me an old post. I cringe at how ignorant I was.

Even now, I don't know the full story of my mother's first marriage. I've never met my two half-brothers. That part of her life is a locked room she rarely enters. I used to think it was shameful, but now I understand it as survival. Some stories are too heavy to retell, especially when you're still carrying them.

My mother's silence taught me a lot. It taught me to read tone instead of words, to observe rather than ask. I became fluent in the emotional language of gestures—a well-timed sigh, a plate set a little harder on the table, a look that lasted too long. That kind of literacy made me hypersensitive to energy, something I carry into every room I enter.

It also made me hesitant to share. As much as I longed to be emotionally open, I learned to wait for the right time—to test the waters before revealing too much. That hesitancy wasn't fear; it was cultural conditioning. Vulnerability felt like an intrusion.

On my father's side, emotions were sometimes explosive. On my mother's side, they were withheld. Somewhere between those two extremes, I tried to carve out my way to feel. To speak. To be.

In Black families, respect is everything. Elders aren't questioned. Privacy isn't just expected—it's enforced. And emotional transparency? It can be seen as weakness, even disrespect. So I grew up carefully managing what I shared, choosing silence when I should have screamed, choosing nods when I needed to ask why.

It wasn't until I had children of my own that I began to understand how deeply that silence shaped me. I saw myself doing the same thing—offering love through acts, not always through words. Holding back tears when I should have let them fall. Dismissing pain instead of naming it.

Now, I try to break that cycle, not by blaming my mother, but by understanding her. She survived what she had to. She gave what she could. And in the quiet, she gave me the tools to build something louder. Something more whole.

My children will know their heritage. Not just through food and holidays, but through stories and honesty. Through the fullness of emotion. Through questions answered. Through hugs that aren't earned, but given freely. I carry my mother's strength in every bone. But I also carry the silence. And it's time to turn some of that silence into voice.

THE BLACKAPINO

My Mother and her first children.

HAIR, IDENTITY, AND THE STRUGGLE FOR ACCEPTANCE

For years, my hair had been a problem. At twelve, I was obsessed with *Power Rangers* and Steven Seagal movies. Both the Green Ranger and Seagal had one thing in common—long hair. That was all the inspiration I needed to start growing mine out. At first, it was just a fun way to switch things up, but soon, it became a source of tension—not just within my family, but with the world around me.

Being mistaken for a girl was something I never expected to deal with. And yet, it happened—more than once.

The first time was at my eighth-grade dance. I was standing around, minding my business, when I felt someone come up behind me, trying to dance. A dude. I jumped away instantly, spinning around to confront whoever had the nerve. The look on his face said it all—pure shock. When he realized I was a guy, he awkwardly laughed it off and apologized, but the damage was done. I felt verbally assaulted, like my identity had been stripped away in a second. My clothes weren't even feminine—so what the hell was it?

The second time was even wilder. I was fifteen, rolling with my best friend, up to no good as usual. We had borrowed—well, stolen—his grandparents' car for the night. He was driving me and this pretty chocolate-skinned girl I'd met at the mall—an Oreo by my standards since she went to a predominantly white school. Everything was cool until we ran a flashing red light.

Then came the sirens.

The cop pulled us over, and the situation could've gone left real quick. We were two underage kids in Montgomery County at midnight, in a car we weren't supposed to have, with a girl in the backseat who probably had no clue what she'd signed up for. The officer made my boy step out for questioning while I sat still, heart pounding, thinking: *This is it. This is how I die.*

Then, out of nowhere, the cop looked at me and asked, "Are you two okay?"—his voice weirdly soft and concerned. Not suspicious. Not aggressive. Just . . . gentle.

"Yes, officer," I said, keeping my voice steady.

After a few more questions, he let us go. Just like that. As soon as we pulled off, my friend burst out laughing. "Yo," he said between breaths, "I think that cop let us go 'cause he thought you were a girl." I was in disbelief. *Again?*

Maybe it was luck. Maybe it was his white privilege. Or maybe—just maybe—it was my damn hair again.

My mom hated my long hair. She was old-school, and in her mind, boys weren't supposed to have ponytails. My brother thought it was cool, but had jokes for days.

"You look like a girl from behind," he'd say, laughing.

It didn't bother me too much—our cousin D had long hair too. The only difference? He had a mustache and a more masculine face.

Still, I didn't cut it. Not until I discovered braids.

My cousin had a friend whose mom, Ms. Linda, could braid hair. The first time I sat in her chair, I had no idea what I was in for. The way she snatched my scalp had me questioning every decision I had made up until that moment. First came the parting—sharp, precise, unforgiving. Then the gel—thick and cold. Finally, the weaving—pulling my hair so tight my scalp felt like it was on fire.

I tried to stay strong, but when she got to the sides? Tears, man. Straight-up tears.

"You tender-headed?" she asked, smirking.

I had no clue what that even meant, but I sure as hell knew I was in pain.

Still, when she finished, I looked in the mirror and saw a brand new me.

The next day at school, people were in awe. They were checking the length, seeing how far my braids went down my neck—because back then, "hang time" mattered. If your braids didn't have length, you weren't doing it right. I had the Allen Iverson effect going.

For a while, this became my signature look. But by ninth grade, I was tired of the upkeep. Braids needed maintenance, washing was a pain, and honestly, I was just ready for something different.

FLAWS-N-ALL, AND
THE ART OF OWNING IT

One of my most loved and hated songs was "Karma Chameleon" by Boy George. My pops used to play it ten times in a row when he was on his Seagram's binge. In an interview, Culture Club's frontman explained: *"The song is about the terrible fear of alienation that people have—the fear of standing up for one thing. It's about trying to suck up to everybody."*

It wasn't until I got older that I understood what he meant.

As I struggled with my racial identity, so much of it was shaped by how I looked to others. *Beauty is in the eye of the beholder*—and I wasn't sure what "beautiful" looked like on me. I was just a 5'6", acne-faced, skinny dude with an Even Steven haircut—another kid trying to figure out where he fit in. Style felt like a guessing game, like building a Sims character with no clue what the final version should look like.

And my mix of friends only made it harder.

MICHAEL GOODLOE

I bounced between two looks: an urban aesthetic—graphic tees, fresh sneakers—or a more polished, preppy style—button-downs and loafers. The problem wasn't the clothes. It was my face. The face card didn't always match the style I was trying to adopt. My features—too smooth, too boyish—left me feeling out of sync with the image I wanted to project. I wanted to look like the grown man I was becoming, but I felt stuck in the awkward limbo of youth.

Everything changed when I landed a decent-paying job. With a little financial freedom, I started taking my grooming and self-presentation seriously. Before the internet became the go-to for everything, I had a subscription to *GQ* magazine. For months, I studied how men with my build, my hair type, my complexion dressed. I took notes. I paid attention to details—fits, textures, accessories.

And as luck would have it, I grew a few more inches, leveling out at 5'10" with a 32L/30W frame. Suddenly, I could pull off styles that once felt out of reach.

Up until then, I'd rocked the same low-cut fade for most of my adult life—mostly because I never understood the value of a good barber.

FINDING THE LOOK AND HOLDING THE LINE

I had always loved gangster films—*Goodfellas, Casino, Scarface*. But it wasn't until I saw *Ocean's Eleven* that I realized hair could be a power move. Every cool, confident, high-status man in those films had one thing in common—a pompadour.

It was clean. Sharp. Controlled. And I wanted in.

I went to the best barber I could find and asked for a low fade with a pompadour. I remember the first time I saw myself in the mirror after styling it at home—fresh out the shower, pomade worked through, hair perfectly in place. I looked like a made man. My jawline looked sharper. My height? Instantly boosted. The whole aesthetic? Old money.

This wasn't just a haircut. It was an identity shift. And people noticed.

The girl I was dating at the time? She fell in love all over again. She'd run her fingers through my hair, rub the back of my head, telling me how much she loved it. It felt like being a damn lapdog getting scratched behind the ears.

I started to see a version of myself that felt intentional. With a manicured cut and a refined wardrobe, I found a style that balanced street edge with grown-man polish. My new look became a blend of fitted chinos, casual sneakers, and a blazer—business casual but with flavor. And with Gucci Mane flooding the industry, I even started accessorizing with jewelry, curating a personal style that felt both effortless and distinct.

I was proud of this new Michael—polished, self-assured, iced out with no stylist.

But of course, with change comes criticism.

The streets had opinions, and they made them known. The word was out: apparently, I looked like Miguel, the R&B singer. It was meant as a compliment, but the hate rolled in just as fast.

"Why you always so dressed up?"

"Bruh, you doing too much."

That hit me differently. I had finally found a style that felt right, but instead of being embraced, I felt othered again. No matter how much I tried to own my uniqueness, people still found a way to make me feel like an outsider. That old insecurity crept back in—the same one I'd carried growing up, being too Black for the Asians and too Asian for the Black kids.

Then I remembered something a friend once told me: "The reason people like you is because you're different. Just be you." So I owned it. Flaws and all.

But the commentary didn't stop—it just shifted. Now that I had a distinct look, people started coming for my hair. After all these

THE BLACKAPINO

years of struggling to define myself, my hair was the new target?

I'd spent most of my life trying to belong—to be Black enough, Filipino enough, street enough, cool enough. But eventually, I realized I didn't have to prove anything to anyone.

Being from the DMV, multiracial folks weren't unheard of. But mixed guys usually had a specific look—a certain texture to their hair, like Patrick Mahomes. Even the Black-and-white mixed dudes still leaned toward the familiar. Me? People saw a Black guy—until they saw my hair.

I had embraced a close-fade pompadour—the best version of what I could do with my fine, straight hair that looked more Chinese than Black. And the reactions were . . . interesting.

One night, I was at Cheeseburger Baby in Miami Beach around 2 AM when none other than *Drink Champs* host N.O.R.E. pulled up. Being the outgoing person I am, I went to introduce myself, and the first thing out of his mouth?

"Damn, that's the greatest conk I ever seen in life!"

I had never heard that word before. I knew it was all love, but it hit me—even in a city full of diversity, my look still stopped people in their tracks. My hair was more than just hair. It was the ultimate symbol of my racial ambiguity, a conversation starter whether I liked it or not.

But over time, I started to see my so-called flaws for what they really were—assets.

My look was universally attractive—not because I was trying to be something I wasn't, but because I had finally grown into myself. The baby face that once made me feel undermined in conversations? Now it worked in my favor. No matter how many birthdays passed, people always assumed I was younger. It used to bother me—made me feel like I wasn't being taken seriously.

But I had to laugh.

Blacks don't crack, and Asians don't age.

By the time I hit my 30s, I looked better than most Gen Z babies. The things that once made me feel out of place now made me stand out—in the best way.

What used to feel like a daily struggle for identity had become a daily reminder of my power—every time I looked in the mirror.

MIXED MEN, MIRROR IMAGES

There's a particular glance we give each other.

Mixed men. Ambiguous men. The ones who know what it means to be asked, "What are you?" before being asked our names.

It's not always verbal. Sometimes it's just a nod across the room, a flicker of recognition. Other times, it carries tension—a silent question of whether this person is a brother in shared experience or a rival navigating the same tightrope.

Growing up, I rarely had mixed male peers. Most of the biracial kids I knew were girls, and they got a different kind of treatment—the kind that assumed beauty and softness. But for us? It was different. Being racially ambiguous as a man wasn't an advantage. It was a constant negotiation. When I did meet another mixed man, I couldn't help but scan for similarities. Did he have the same features people fixated on in me? Did he code-switch the way I did? Did he carry himself like he belonged—or like he was trying to belong?

There was camaraderie, yes. But sometimes, it came with competition. Because there's only so much room in people's understanding of what mixed masculinity looks like. And when that space is limited, it becomes a silent contest: Who fits the mold better? Who gets accepted faster? Who gets seen first?

Just like the time I met a fellow Blasian at my cousin's house one night—he worked at the commissary on Fort Meade. I should mention, being a bagger at The Commissary back in the day was the job to have. It was guaranteed cash. Military families tipped heavily, especially on the weekends, and the young guys who worked there had a certain unspoken status.

That night, he rolled in with a few of his homeboys—Baltimore types, I suspected, since my cousin went to Meade High in Anne Arundel County. We were all chatting when my cousin threw out the fact that I could rap a little. Immediately, dude cut his eyes at me. He was trying to see what I was about—if I was real or just talk. I gave a quick profile: I was from Laurel. PG County.

Then the debate started. Anne Arundel versus PG County. The subtle one-upmanship that isn't really about geography—it's about identity. Authenticity. Belonging.

There was one thing he said that stuck with me. He looked straight at me and said, "It's not where you're from, it's where you be at."

I couldn't argue with that. It was truth. In seconds, he'd done something I'd spent years trying to explain—he showed up fully himself. No flex. No need to prove anything. That moment humbled me. I realized we were both trying to size each other up, when we should've been seeing ourselves reflected.

In high school and early adulthood, I found myself gravitating toward other racially ambiguous men. Sometimes we clicked instantly. We could speak in shorthand, joke about how our moms raised us to eat with our hands. Our sense of fashion by complimenting each other by the choice of shoes or shirt we have on. That shorthand was sacred. It was relief. It was real.

But not every encounter felt like brotherhood. There were times I met someone like me, and instead of a connection, I felt scrutiny. Like we were sizing each other up. Like only one of us could be the "right" kind of mixed in a given circle. It was subtle. Sometimes it showed up in who got invited where. Other times, it was in how people compared us out loud, as if we were auditioning for the same role in someone else's script.

That kind of tension isn't always about ego. Sometimes it's about fear—the fear that if someone else embodies your ambiguity differently, you might get erased. That you might be seen as less than, less Black, less Filipino, less valid. And when your whole identity already exists in a fragile balance, that fear cuts deep.

Social media didn't help. It turned identity into branding. Suddenly, biracial men were showing up on curated explore pages, posted for their "unique" looks. But that visibility didn't always feel like progress. It felt like packaging. Marketable ambiguity. The kind that didn't come with our history, our confusion, our stories.

That's when I realized: not all mixed men are created equal in the eyes of the world. Some are welcomed into certain rooms. Others are questioned, sidelined, even envied. And the only thing separating us is how readable our ambiguity is. How easily people can place us, claim us, explain us.

But the most meaningful connections I've had with other mixed men weren't about image or approval. They happened in quiet conversations—in barbershops, over drinks, in the kitchen of someone's kickback. When the walls came down and we talked about what it really meant to grow up in between.

How our dads taught us strength, but not softness.

How our moms gave us culture, but not always language.

How we got used to playing translator—not just between ethnicities, but between versions of ourselves.

We talked about relationships. About being fetishized, misunderstood, and misnamed. About feeling like we had to be exceptional just to be accepted. About how exhausting it was to be everyone's safe bet, everyone's blank slate.

Those conversations reminded me that intersectional belonging isn't just about being mixed. It's about how you carry it. How do you connect through it? How do you resist the urge to compete to feel whole?

I still catch myself in those glances, those half-nods across the room. Still wondering: Are you like me? Do you get it? Can we talk?

And more often than not, the answer is yes. Because under the performance, under the posturing, under the polished ambiguity—there's a shared knowing. And in that knowing, we belong.

THE BLACKAPINO

Me, DiCarie and Aaron

RELATIONSHIPS

Let's be blunt—dating is a battlefield. And for someone like me, the terrain is even trickier to navigate. I don't have the luxury of falling back on the idea that, if all else fails, I'll just "end up with my people." Because, truthfully, *who are my people?*

If you don't believe me, think about that one white girl you knew growing up—the one who only dated Black guys in high school, swore up and down that was her type. Then years later, you check Facebook, and there she is—married with kids to a white guy.

People love to talk about being open-minded, but when it comes to choosing a partner for the long haul, most retreat to what's familiar. It's like a survival instinct—whether they admit it or not. Just look around. Most couples you see mirror each other.

And if that weren't true, why would we have entire studies tracking who marries who, which groups are thriving in the dating market, and which are struggling?

Logically speaking, the odds are already stacked against me.

The problem with being a biracial man is you don't fit neatly into anyone's type. Biracial women? Society puts them on a pedestal, often exoticizing their look into desirability. But for men like me? There's no universal appeal—just confusion.

As a heterosexual, Black and Filipino man, I learned early that my appearance alone could throw people off. No shade to the LGBTQ community, but Filipino men don't have the most masculine reputation—at least not in the American dating market. If you don't believe me, watch that *Family Guy* episode where Brian's gay cousin shows up with his Filipino boyfriend. The stereotype is right there—played for laughs.

And it wasn't just women making assumptions. Gay men often mistook me for one of their own—not because of how I acted, but because of how I looked. They saw a Black guy with perfectly permed-looking hair, well-groomed, put-together—and in their minds, that had to mean I was gay. It didn't matter that I was just a meticulous dude who cared about his appearance. The standard for masculinity showed its ugly face—being too well-groomed was a red flag. Men were supposed to be rugged, effortlessly handsome, never *too* polished.

That was my introduction to how much appearance shapes perception.

Being well-groomed and well-spoken—qualities that *should* be assets—often felt like liabilities. Women want a man who takes care of himself, sure. But there's a fine line between "well-kept" and "too pretty." And apparently, I was walking it.

Women would tell me they preferred a man who looked like he could fix a car, not one who just took good Instagram photos. Never mind that I was plenty capable of getting my hands dirty—I just didn't *look* the part.

And it wasn't just my appearance—it was how I spoke.

One night, after leaving a club in Baltimore, I walked up to a woman I found attractive. Before I could even finish a sentence, she gave me a look—like she was still trying to decide if I was even attractive. Then she hit me with: "You sound too proper."

There it was—that unspoken cultural test. I knew exactly what she meant. That "white-sounding" voice—too polished, too articulate, too far removed from the local Baltimore or D.C. dialect. Never mind that I knew the slang, that I *grew up* around Black culture. To her, I didn't sound like I belonged.

I'll be real—back then, the environment was wild. Especially around spots like Hammerjacks. The night scene in Baltimore was rowdy and unpredictable. Most guys were, for lack of a better word, hood. Maybe if I'd approached her with less etiquette and more arrogance, the outcome would've been different.

I started noticing a pattern. Most of my boys had no issue dating within their race. They didn't have to think about this stuff—how their looks, their voice, or their racial background might be affecting their dating pool. They had a clear lane.

Black guys dated Black women. Asian guys dated Asian women.

And while they could coach me on confidence or game, they couldn't relate to *my* struggle—the struggle of never being "enough" of anything.

THE MISUNDERSTOOD MIDDLE

Even when I turned to my own family for insight, I hit a dead end. It was a lonely feeling—and pride kept me from asking for help. Guys don't usually put much emphasis on race. Women do. We're simple: if she's checking for me, I'm checking for her.

Most of my biracial cousins exclusively dated Black partners. Even my female cousins, who were also Black and Filipino, seemed to have an easier time being accepted within the Black dating scene. It wasn't just a preference—it was the path of least resistance. If I asked them what worked for them, they probably wouldn't even understand the question—because they never had to question it in the first place.

So where did that leave me?

It wasn't that I couldn't get dates. My experience in the dating world wasn't one of rejection—it was one of constant misinterpretation. When I dated Black women, I often felt a stronger connection because I was raised in a predominantly Black cultural atmosphere.

They seemed more accepting of my identity than other groups. But even then, I couldn't shake the feeling that I was sometimes seen as an experiment—something "different" to try.

And when it came to dating outside my race? Those experiences often felt . . . transactional.

Before social media gave us unlimited access to people from different backgrounds, this kind of thinking wasn't as obvious. But the more I paid attention, the more I started to wonder: was I being appreciated for who I was—or just for what I represented?

Over time, I noticed a trend. My biracial cousin—also half Black and Filipino—had a completely different experience. White women were drawn to him.

Why?

We had similar features, similar upbringings. But looking back, I realized environment made all the difference. I was raised in a predominantly Black space, which gave me confidence in dating Black women. He, on the other hand, was more embedded in white social circles.

Was it how we carried ourselves? The cultural references we understood? Or was it something deeper—something about how different racial identities are perceived in dating?

Growing up, the only widely recognized biracial Black and Asian man in pop culture was Tiger Woods. He was the exception, not the rule. It wasn't until the late 2000s and into the 2020s that men who looked like me started to become more visible. And even then, biracial women still had it easier.

I found some clarity after one relationship—a woman I dated a few years after high school. She was Black and Caribbean, from

St. Thomas, and she embraced everything about me that I once second-guessed.

She told me: "You don't look like anyone I've ever dated—and that's what I like about you."

That stuck with me. Because for once, my differences weren't seen as a problem. They were an asset.

In public, people would compliment us as a couple, saying we looked good together. And she made it clear: my appearance, my voice, my energy—none of it needed to be altered to be attractive. It was the validation I didn't even realize I needed.

But dating isn't just about looks.

Once I was in a relationship, I faced a different challenge:

How was I supposed to act?

I started noticing that who I was around influenced how I carried myself. When I dated women with strong, assertive personalities, I sometimes felt the need to match that energy—especially with PG County girls, who had a reputation for being more aggressive. But when I was in Northern Virginia, where the women were more culturally fluid, I didn't feel that same pressure.

I wasn't faking it, but I was definitely adjusting—code-switching without even realizing it.

One weekend, I could be at an urban nightclub, effortlessly engaging women in conversation. The next, I'd be at Pub Dog—a bar my white friends loved—where I had to calculate my interactions more carefully. One wrong joke, one misunderstood cultural reference, and suddenly I was the "other."

At some point, I had to ask myself: "Was I shaping my dating life around other people's?"

The answer was yes.

I had been so caught up trying to fit into different spaces that I hadn't realized how much I was bending—and for what? When I met the woman who would later become the mother of my child, I posed a question I had once asked on social media: "Would dating a biracial man be considered dating outside your race?"

Her answer? "You're not who I'd typically date."

It wasn't a rejection—just an observation. She'd been raised in a predominantly Black area, and I was the first man outside that comfort zone she'd ever been with.

But as our relationship grew, I realized something important:

It wasn't about changing myself to fit into someone's world.

It was about finding someone who saw value in what made me different.

And maybe, just maybe, that was the real key to breaking the cycle.

WHAT WAS MISSING

One thing I've had a bittersweet time accepting is that I never seriously pursued a relationship with an Asian woman. Not by conscious choice—just because the opportunity never really presented itself. Not even a Filipino woman—someone who shared my own racial background.

For a long time, I wondered why.

It didn't take much digging to figure it out. Many Asian women viewed dating a Black man as a step down in social status. The stereotypes weren't subtle. Whether in America or abroad, Black men were often seen as second-class citizens—unstable partners or bad investments for a stable future. The unspoken message was clear: if they wanted to "marry up," they looked to white men.

And I felt that every time I interacted with Asian women.

There was never open hostility—just quiet dismissal. A lack of curiosity. If I did meet an Asian woman I found attractive, I could feel the disconnect before a word was even exchanged. Their eyes were set elsewhere. And I knew better than to take it personally.

The same was true for half-Black, half-Filipino women. In theory, we should've been each other's first and most natural match—same mixed identity, same cultural touch points. But in reality, there was an unspoken taboo. If you were half-Black and half-Filipino, dating someone of the same mix felt too close to home.

The running joke was always: "Aren't we probably related?" The funny thing is—I understood that logic. Growing up, the Filipino side of my family operated like an expansive, informal kinship network. We called people "cousins" even when there was no actual blood relation. It was normal to walk into a Filipino gathering and hear, "Oh, that's your cousin." And you just accepted it. No questions asked.

That sense of closeness made the idea of dating someone with my exact mix feel too familiar—almost incestuous—even when we weren't related at all.

So there I was—disconnected from one side of my racial identity when it came to dating. And even if the stigma wasn't there, most of the half-Filipino, half-Black women I knew were into Black men. I never saw them dating white men, and their social circles reflected that same preference.

My girlfriend had a similar experience growing up in a predominantly Black space. But being a biracial man and being a biracial woman are not equal struggles. Women—especially in Black culture—are often celebrated for their racial ambiguity. Exoticized, even. I'd seen it firsthand. My female cousins, also half-Black and half-Filipino, never had to question their desirability. Men of all backgrounds found them attractive.

Biracial men? We don't always get that same admiration.

So in a way, I understood why the half-Black, half-Filipino women I knew felt more at home dating Black men. They weren't being forced to prove anything. They didn't have to explain themselves.

Me? I was still searching for that same ease.

THE ALGORITHM OF LOVE

Dating in the 2020s is like stepping into a digital marketplace, where people aren't looking for love so much as they're curating the perfect match. Algorithms and automation have made dating feel more like shopping for a custom-built car than forming a real connection. Movies like *I, Robot* and *The Terminator* once seemed like distant fiction, but now—with the way tech dictates our lives, including how we fall in love—that reality feels closer than ever.

I wasn't immune to the shift. Dating apps became a battlefield. And my biggest opponent? My racial identity.

The options were simple: Black, White, Asian, Hispanic. As if those four boxes could capture the depth of a person's heritage. I often wondered: *Where does someone like me fit?* I wasn't just Black. I wasn't just Asian. And in a world where first impressions are made in half a second on a swipe, nuance didn't matter.

It wasn't just about which apps I used—it was about who those apps were *for*. The mainstream platforms like Tinder, Plenty of Fish, and Match.com felt like first-world dating experiences, built around people who already had a preset mold of what they wanted. I rarely fit that mold.

My best shot at success came with apps geared toward Black culture, like Soul Swipe or BLK—places where I at least had a better chance of being *seen*.

But even then, the whole thing felt mechanical. A digital profile couldn't capture who I really was. The rhythm of conversation was different—awkward, forced, and easily abandoned. People ghosted at the slightest inconvenience, hiding behind screens instead of navigating the real flow of human connection.

Still, I was persistent.

And that persistence eventually led me to the mother of my child.

Our first real conversation lasted over three hours on the phone. I've always been a talker—able to string words together in a way that makes people comfortable. That night, we traded stories like old friends catching up. I laid out my whole life, including my past relationship and the fact that I had a child. I expected hesitation—maybe even judgment. But instead, she understood. She'd grown up in a similar situation, shaped by the absence of her own biological parents.

Our first date was in Washington, DC, at the infamous Ming's Chinese Restaurant in Gallery Place. I don't remember exactly what I wore, but I know I had that shit on.

She got there first. And like a nervous girl playing it cool, she pretended to be in the bathroom—probably peeking out to make sure I wasn't a catfish. When I arrived, I texted her that I was sitting by the window. Seconds later, my future baby mama appeared—

grinning, open-armed, sliding into the seat across from me like we'd done this a thousand times before.

That night was a blur of good conversation and easy laughter. Afterward, we went back to her place, smoked, and let the night settle around us.

By the second or third date, we had sex.

That's when things got complicated.

A LOVE THAT NEVER SETTLED

Our relationship was a rollercoaster—passionate, volatile, unpredictable. Some days, we were inseparable. Other days, we were at each other's throats. Looking back, I think we both wanted something stable, but we were too different—or maybe too similar in all the wrong ways.

A month into dating, she invited me to a family cookout. At the time, it felt almost too soon. I didn't realize how big her family was until I walked through that door. The moment I stepped in, I was met with curious smiles and that classic *"Who's this guy?"* energy.

In my head, I laughed, thinking of the classic Black family joke—when an uncle sees the new boyfriend and hits him with the: "I see you, nephew."

I never asked about the men she'd dated before me, but I had a feeling none of them looked like me. Even now, years later, I'll meet friends or relatives of hers for the first time and can see it in their faces—the curiosity, the confusion, the quiet: *"Wait, this is the guy?"*

One moment that stuck with me was meeting one of her friend's uncles. He stared at me for a good ten seconds before blurting out: "You look like one of them dudes from *The Five Heartbeats*!"

He meant it as a compliment. I was wearing a scarf around my head and a three-quarter-length peacoat, channeling that old-school, smooth look. Older Black folks always saw something familiar in me. The way I carried myself reminded them of the era when Black men permed their hair, dressed sharp, and exuded a certain kind of quiet power.

Even barbers noticed it. At Barbers of St. James, one of the older heads once told me I reminded him of a famous Black singer from the '50s. I had a throwback aesthetic that resonated with their generation—even though, ironically, it sometimes made me feel out of place in my own.

My relationship with my daughter's mother wasn't perfect, but she *got* me in a way few others did. She had this relentless curiosity about my Asian heritage—almost like she was trying to draw something out of me that I had buried.

She loved seafood and Asian cuisine, always pushing us to try new restaurants or nudging me to learn how to cook real Filipino food. Funny thing was, despite being half-Filipino, I'd never been that deep into the culture. She, on the other hand, was fascinated by it.

Ironic, isn't it? The woman I had a child with was the one encouraging me to embrace a part of myself I had long overlooked. Maybe that was the best and worst part of us—we challenged each other, but we also exhausted each other.

Looking back, I don't think we ever stood a chance at being forever. But we were *meant* to cross paths. She gave me my daughter.

She made me see myself in ways I hadn't before. And in a world where dating had become a numbers game, she was proof that sometimes the most meaningful connections can't be calculated by an algorithm.

THE WEIGHT OF YOUNG LOVE

Before my daughter's mother, my first serious relationship came in my early 20s. I was still immature, still figuring out who I was, and still making decisions driven more by lust than wisdom.

That's the thing about being young and open to love—you make mistakes without even realizing it. And in my case, the mistake wasn't just about choosing the wrong person. It was not knowing *myself* well enough to choose better.

That mistake took the form of a relationship with my son's mother—a woman I met in the same neighborhood where I lived.

If there's one piece of advice I could give my younger self, it's this:

Never date someone who lives where you do.

When you need peace and quiet, you get disruption. When you crave space, it's nowhere to be found.

I never asked her what she saw in me, but I don't think it was about love—it was about comfort. She had just moved in with her sister and was looking for familiarity in a new place. Maybe I represented security. Companionship. A buffer from loneliness.

She was from Pennsylvania, a self-described Oreo—Black on the outside, but "white" in how she spoke and carried herself. Most of her friends were white, and her lively personality always set her apart. But underneath all that energy was something heavier—a family history I never took the time to fully understand.

Her family was Liberian. She had been raised in a house full of relatives after losing her mother. Her father had been unfaithful, and those fractured relationships shaped how she viewed love.

At the time, I didn't know how to process that. I didn't stop to think how her upbringing shaped her expectations, her insecurities, or her deep need for connection. I was just going with the flow, assuming that love—or at least the idea of it—would smooth over the cracks.

I realize now, I should've paid more attention. I should've asked:

Am I forcing this to work? Am I trying to change someone into who I want them to be?

But I was young and reckless, chasing a feeling without considering the consequences.

THE ILLUSION OF STABILITY

A year in, we moved in together—not far from our families, but far enough to convince ourselves we were building something of our own.

Truth is, I wasn't ready.

I liked the *idea* of having my own place. But I still wanted freedom. I was the first in my crew to move in with a girl, but I was still trying to hang like I was single. My boys weren't tied down. They could go out whenever they wanted—and I wanted to be right there with them.

But when you play house, reality checks in fast. Not long after we moved in, she got pregnant. I was terrified.

I had no idea how to be a father. I didn't know how my parents would react. I had always assumed I'd do things in the "right" order—marriage first, then kids. But there I was: unmarried, with a baby on the way, and no blueprint.

My parents weren't angry. But they were shocked. Maybe they

saw it coming before I did. Maybe they knew I wasn't as grown as I thought I was. At the time, I thought it was a curse. What I didn't realize was that my son—this child I wasn't ready for—would become my greatest blessing.

Ten months after my son was born, my world changed again. My brother died. We had shared the same room for over twenty years—laughing, fighting, growing up side by side. And just like that, he was gone.

I had spent so much time fearing fatherhood, worried about how it would change me, that I didn't even realize how much I was about to lose.

Suddenly, my son wasn't just a responsibility. He was a lifeline. In the same way I grew up alongside my brother, I now had to raise a child of my own. I used to think parenthood was something you *prepared* for. That you figured it out *before* it happened.

But life doesn't wait. It throws you in the fire—and makes you grow. I was still young, still flawed, still learning. But for the first time in my life, I had something that mattered more than myself.

MY FIRST BEST FRIEND

My brother and I were born just a year apart, close enough in age that our lives felt intertwined. His name was Aaron William Goodloe, an iteration of our father's name, Ronald William Goodloe. In many ways, he was my reflection—someone who understood me without needing words—but he was also his own force, someone I admired deeply.

Unfortunately, Aaron's life was shaped by a battle we both knew too well: hemoglobin E beta thalassemia.

We were hospital kids.

But while I had a milder form, he bore the brunt of it. His life revolved around monthly blood transfusions, and sometimes he had to stay overnight for monitoring. He had a port installed beneath his collarbone—a permanent access point for those transfusions. For him, it was just normal. For me, it was a constant reminder that my big brother carried a burden I didn't.

But you wouldn't have known it by looking at him.

Aaron was fearless. Despite the limitations of his health, he never let it define him. He bloomed earlier than I did—more confident, more self-assured, more magnetic. If I was still figuring out who I was, he had already claimed his space in the room.

We had the same mixed-race features, but he leaned more toward our mother—boxier face, stronger jawline. He blended in easily with the neighborhood kids. They were his age, his grade. I was the tag along, always a step behind, hoping to catch some of his confidence by proximity.

THE RACIAL DIVIDE BETWEEN US

Even though we shared the same parents, house, and bloodline, the world didn't see us the same.

Aaron leaned more Filipino in his features—slightly lighter skin, a face that people could categorize more easily. I, on the other hand, had a look that made people pause.

"What are you?"

I got that question all the time. Aaron? Rarely.

Maybe it was because he didn't care. Or maybe it was because he fit into people's assumptions more comfortably. But for me, there was always this tension—this sense that I had to explain myself in ways he never had to.

People would ask if we were cousins. Or say, "Y'all got different dads?" It was funny at first. Then it got old.

How could someone who shared my blood feel like a racial outlier in my own story?

Aaron never second-guessed his place. He fit in with the Black kids, the Filipino kids, the mixed kids—anyone. He wore confidence like a second skin. The way he talked, the way he dressed, the way people gravitated toward him—it all came so naturally.

Me? I was more cautious. I scanned the room first. Measured my words. Tried to figure out which version of myself was "right" for the space.

Aaron's racial identity was never a topic. Mine was always a conversation. Even women treated us differently.

Aaron didn't have to explain himself. He had that instant pull that bypassed questions. I had to be decoded. I was "exotic." "Interesting." Sometimes "too different." He was accepted on sight. I had to be explained. Girls loved him.

It didn't matter what race they were—they came to him.

Some guys learn how to talk to women; others just have an energy that pulls them in. Aaron was one of those guys. Maybe it was the long hair he grew after high school, maybe it was the way he carried himself—bold, effortless, like he had nothing to prove. I, on the other hand, felt like I was still waiting for my turn. If he had a full cup of game, mine was only half full.

He had a style I took for granted early on—always dressed sharp, always put together. While I was still figuring out what worked for me, he already had it mastered. And yet, despite our differences, we were inseparable.

Funny enough, we never really talked about race. Not in a deep way, at least. Aaron just lived in his skin. He wasn't oblivious, but he also didn't dwell on it. If a girl liked him, she liked him. If people accepted him, they accepted him. Simple. But me? I carried those questions everywhere.

I wanted to talk about it, to break it down, to make sense of why things felt different for me. But those conversations never really happened. Maybe because Aaron didn't feel that struggle the same way. Maybe because he didn't need to. And that's what I envied about him. He never had to prove anything.

MY BROTHERS KEEPER

Every move I made, he was the one setting up the journey.

Some of my best memories are of us taking late-night drives, windows down, music playing, just existing in the same space. We didn't need to talk about anything deep—the silence was never uncomfortable. That was the thing about having an older brother you were close to—he wasn't just my sibling; he was my first best friend.

We lived the same life. We experienced the same things. But what made it fun was that we never told the same story.

Aaron had a way of exaggerating everything—turning the smallest moment into an epic saga. We could have gone through the exact same situation, but when he told it, it was always bigger, crazier, more dramatic. That's what made our conversations exciting. I never knew how he'd spin it, but I always knew I'd be entertained.

When he passed, it felt like an entire piece of my life had been erased. But it wasn't just his absence that I felt—it was the way the world around me changed. Without him, I lost the one person who made me feel grounded in my own family.

The people we knew, the mutual friends we shared—they started to drift away. Some out of grief, some out of discomfort, some because maybe, without Aaron, our bond wasn't as strong as we thought. The dynamics shifted, and I had to learn how to navigate life without my built-in guide.

Losing a brother isn't just losing family—it's losing a witness to your life. Someone who could finish your sentences. Someone who could remind you of things you forgot. Someone who saw you from the beginning, in every phase, in every version of yourself.

If Aaron were here today, he'd have so much more to share. And you know what? His version of this story would probably be way better than mine.

It's hard to say whether my relationships with the mothers of my children reflect good or bad choices. Maybe that's the wrong way to frame it—because in the end, they were never just choices. They were moments of discovery, lessons that shaped the man I became. But they also forced me to confront something deeper: how my racial ambiguity influenced the way I was seen, and ultimately, how I saw myself in love and relationships.

I never went into relationships with a clear plan. Commitment always felt like something I was supposed to want, but not something I fully embraced. Maybe it was because I liked my freedom, or maybe it was because I always felt like I was navigating relationships from the outside looking in. Either way, I was moving through relationships like a man who thought he was a catch but wasn't sure if he wanted to be caught. My mixed identity complicated things in ways I didn't always recognize at the time. It wasn't just about preference—it was about perception. How women saw me. How I saw myself in relation to them.

By all accounts, I should have been the ideal partner—well-rounded, stable career, ambitious. But relationships aren't just about credentials. They require presence, patience, and a willingness to build with someone, not just exist beside them. And in my early twenties, I wasn't ready for that truth. Maybe part of that was because I didn't fully know where I fit. I wasn't always seen as "Black enough" or "Asian enough" to fit neatly into someone's ideal partner.

If Kevin Samuels had been around when I was navigating relationships, I might have moved differently. He was a highly influential and polarizing figure for Black male culture during the pandemic before his passing in May of 2022. He was a self-described image consultant and YouTube personality who gained notoriety for his blunt, often controversial commentary on dating, gender roles, and self-improvement— especially within the Black community. Even though his tactics were divisive, Kevin Samuels sparked essential conversations about self-perception, dating standards, and gender dynamics. Maybe I would've been more strategic, more guarded, more focused on myself before entertaining commitment. Some may disagree with that sentiment, but there's something to be said about timing and self-awareness. Understanding your social currency. And being biracial in a world that often demands clear-cut identities meant that I wasn't always sure how I was valued in the dating market.

Looking back, I wonder: If I had prioritized myself instead of relationships, would things have turned out differently? Would I have built a stronger foundation for myself before trying to build with someone else? It's easy to say "what if," but I can't dwell on that.

Because the truth is, my relationships—flawed as they were—shaped my journey. They brought me to places I never expected, introduced me to people who changed my path, and forced me to confront who I was beyond my own expectations. My belief in community, connection, and experience kept me moving, even when love didn't go the way I thought it would.

Maybe, in the end, it wasn't about the relationships themselves, but about who I became because of them. And maybe, just maybe, part of that journey was realizing that my racial ambiguity wasn't just something I had to explain or justify in love—it was something I had to embrace within myself first.

WORKPLACE DISCOURSE

I live with this lingering regret that I never attended a traditional four-year college. It's not just about the degree—it's about the access, the networks, and the unspoken advantages that come with that experience. Deep down, I believe that if I had gone, I would have had an even more successful career, one where I navigated both personal and professional diversity with greater strategy and foresight. Maybe I would have been more prepared for the subtleties of corporate culture, the coded language, the politics of being a person of color in predominantly white spaces.

But it's too late to cry over spilled milk. And truth be told, I'm grateful for the success I've carved out—on my own terms. What's interesting about my career is that I didn't just work in my field—I moved through every level of it. I found myself in rooms that many would consider out of reach for someone without a graduate degree—let alone someone like me. I've worked for some of the most prestigious companies in the world, advancing in ways that didn't seem statistically likely for a Black and Filipino man without traditional credentials.

So how was this possible? What set me apart from all the other applicants who had equal or better qualifications?

Experience is everything, sure—but we all know that in most cases, the piece of paper—the degree—is what gets you to the table before you even have a chance to speak. So what got *me* in the door? Was it talent? Adaptability? Or was it something more complicated—my identity, my racial ambiguity, and the way I was perceived by decision-makers?

I often wonder whether my appearance—and the assumptions people made about my background—played a role in my career trajectory. Did hiring managers see me as a diversity win? Someone who could check a box without disrupting the status quo? Or did my ambiguous features make me "safe" enough to bypass the biases that keep so many qualified Black candidates from getting a fair shot?

I never had the luxury of leaning on a single identity in professional spaces. Too Black in some rooms. Not Black enough in others. Filipino, but rarely recognized as such unless I pointed it out. That duality shaped not just how I saw myself—but how others decided my professional worth.

I don't say this to diminish the work I put in. I *earned* my place. But I'd be lying if I said race, perception, and subtle privilege didn't play a role. Because in the corporate world—especially for someone like me—those things are *always* in play.

And living in that in-between space meant navigating my career in ways I'm still unpacking.

As I evolved and gained a deeper understanding of cultural

nuance, I came across a term that finally captured an aspect of my personality I'd never quite been able to explain: *code-switching*.

If you Google it, you'll find that it was first coined in the 1950s by linguist Einar Haugen to describe the practice of shifting between languages in multilingual communities. But the way I understand it—and the way it's lived, especially in Black spaces—is different. It's less academic and more survival tactic. Urban Dictionary nailed it when it framed code-switching as something Black people do to navigate social spaces, often to soften their Blackness in order to be accepted.

For me, it was never something I consciously chose. It was instinct—fluid, automatic. A part of me adapted to my environment without effort. I didn't just change how I sounded; I changed how I flowed. One moment I was quoting *Clueless*—"like, totally"—and the next, I was channeling Bishop from *Juice*. It wasn't mimicry. It was survival. It was strategy.

The best example of this today? Druski. That man's sketches are a masterclass in modern-day code-switching. Through comedy, he's carved out space for people like me who shape-shift depending on the room. Watching him feels like watching my younger self—putting on different social masks to blend in, be liked, or stay safe.

Code-switching, for me, was like having a Swiss Army knife of vernacular—equal parts SAT words and street slang. And if I'm honest, it became a kind of superpower. But I often wonder: was I adapting, or was I hiding? Was I learning to move fluidly between worlds, or was I being molded by everyone else's expectations?

The answer is probably both.

THE BURDEN AND PRIVILEGE OF AMBIGUITY IN THE WORKPLACE

As a white-collar professional in one of the most powerful cities in the world, I've always felt the weight of competition. Washington, DC is where power and opportunity collide—but access isn't always equal. The corporate world here is massive. From *Fortune 500* companies to government contractors, everyone's fighting for talent. And in my fifteen years as a subject matter expert in workplace and facility operations, I've competed against every Tom, Steve, and Joe—a sea of white men who fit the traditional mold of leadership.

I learned early on: perception is everything.

I remember one of my first high-profile interviews. I was suited up, résumé polished, credentials tight. But when I walked in, I saw it—the subtle double take from the hiring manager. The hesitation behind the handshake. They'd read my résumé. They knew I had the experience. But I could tell I didn't match the image they had built in their head.

Was it my skin tone? My last name? The way I spoke?

That moment set the tone for the rest of my career: the silent, unspoken question always hanging in the air—"What are you?"

Most of my interviews, most of the decision-makers I've had to impress, have been white males. That never outwardly bothered me—but I always knew the game. In many cases, I was being hired to do the behind-the-scenes work. The "dirty laundry." I was expected to handle the tasks they didn't want to deal with. Clean up the messes. Smooth over conflicts. Keep things running seamlessly—so they could take the credit.

There's an inside joke I have with a friend: "In the workplace, you can get Michael—or you can get Mr. Goodloe."

Most days, I operate as Mr. Goodloe. Polished. Disciplined. Committed. Following the same "work hard, play hard" code my father and the men before him lived by.

But what does that really mean—for someone like me?

When you're a first- or second-level manager, you're expected to be the bridge. The buffer between leadership and labor. In a workforce as diverse as DC, it only makes sense to hire someone who can make different groups feel comfortable. And that's where my racial ambiguity became both a tool and a burden.

I was just Black enough to connect with other minorities. I could relate. I could communicate. I was the "cool" manager who understood cultural nuance. I'll never forget one conversation with a white executive after a big leadership meeting. He pulled me aside, gave me a firm handshake, and said: "You know, you have a way of making people feel at ease. You're articulate, well-mannered, sharp. People listen to you." I knew what he meant.

I was just Black enough to relate to the Black and brown employees—but *palatable* enough to never make white executives uncomfortable. My *softer* Blackness made me digestible. A non-threatening form of diversity that looked progressive on paper without disrupting the power structure in the room.

He never said it outright. But I felt it. I *knew* it. And yet, among some of my Black colleagues, my presence was seen as a contradiction. How dare I be young, qualified, and well-spoken? How dare I enter rooms they had been denied or had to fight twice as hard to get into?

Especially when many of them were twice my age—seasoned professionals—who had been overlooked for roles I seemed to walk into. I remember the side-eyes. The subtle shade. The unspoken tests of authenticity.

Was I "Black enough"? Did I understand the struggle? Or was I just another corporate puppet—a "diversity hire" there to make the company look good? They saw it right away—I wasn't "100% Black."

And for some, that made my success suspect.

There was always an unspoken expectation that I'd be the workplace asshole. The one who enforced policy. Managed people like numbers. Played the corporate game with no emotion.

But what they didn't see was the tightrope I walked—every single day. I was constantly negotiating who I needed to be in any given moment.

Black enough, but not too Black.

Tough, but not threatening.

Qualified, but not intimidating.

I had to read the room before I even entered it. Adjust my tone. Control my body language. Soften my facial expressions. I wasn't just performing in meetings—I was performing all day. I wasn't just navigating projects and deadlines. I was navigating *perception*.

CODE-SWITCHING AS SURVIVAL

Racial ambiguity and workplace dynamics weren't new to me. They didn't start in the boardroom. I'd been code-switching long before I ever wore a suit.

As a kid, I learned to adjust my voice, my presence, my entire energy depending on who was in the room. The ace up my sleeve was always being both book-smart and street-smart—able to move between communities with ease. I could talk KPIs and metrics with C-level execs in the morning, then chop it up with the janitorial crew by lunch.

That flexibility became my strength. My currency.

But I always knew the game.

Anyone can call a spade a spade—until a big joker hits the table and the house rules were never explained.

The corporate world had its own unspoken expectations, and I mastered the art of playing within them. Speaking politically correct around my white colleagues came naturally because I understood the comfort they needed. They weren't looking to be challenged; they wanted validation that their worldview was the default.

So I gave them what they expected: high-level conversations about business issues, water cooler talk about golf and weekend plans, an agreeable presence that didn't disrupt the hierarchy.

I knew my presence was disarming. My racial ambiguity softened any preconceived fears they might've had about a Black man in management. My tone was measured, my delivery confident but never aggressive. I navigated workplace conflicts with calculated diplomacy, always keeping emotions in check. I had mastered the art of appearing rational instead of reactive, diplomatic instead of defiant.

But behind that strategy was a quiet resentment I couldn't always silence.

Even with all my strategy, I found myself navigating a different kind of expectation—one that came from below, from peers and subordinates.

Because I didn't fit neatly into a racial category, people projected their own assumptions onto me. Some colleagues—especially those from marginalized backgrounds—saw me as a safe space. They confided in me, leaned on me, expected me to co-sign their frustrations. And while I connected with them personally, that comfort zone became a slippery slope.

Professional boundaries blurred into cultural obligations.

A struggling employee might expect leniency because we shared an unspoken understanding of what it felt like to be overlooked. Office gossip found its way to me, because people assumed I'd be in on it—another outsider in a world run by insiders.

My ability to create a comfort zone became both a privilege

and a burden.

But I couldn't blame them. I *understood* that anxiety. The stress of being watched, underestimated, or excluded based on race, gender, or job title. I'd lived it. The difference? I had an added layer—an identity that wasn't easily defined. They didn't share the experience of being *questioned*, *categorized*, or *mistaken*. They didn't know what it was like to be a chameleon by necessity.

And that was the line between us. They sought comfort in solidarity. I had spent my life tightrope-walking between worlds—never fully belonging, but always knowing how to navigate them.

GOOGLE: A CASE STUDY IN AMBIGUITY

I often reflect on past workplace conversations and wonder—did my words ever spark real change? Did my presence shift anyone's perspective? Did I leave a mark?

These questions linger, especially when I think back to one of the most pivotal chapters in my career—my four years at Google.

In 2017, my career catapulted when I was hired as a Workplace Experience Manager at Google's DC office. The role looked simple on paper but was layered in practice. I was the go-to for all things office-related, responsible for ensuring that the workspace ran seamlessly for some of the most powerful legal and policy minds in the country.

This wasn't the hoodie-wearing, sneaker-sporting tech culture you'd find in Mountain View. This was Google DC—corporate bros, Ivy League resumes, pencil skirts cut too sharp, and handshakes that didn't reach the eyes. Passive-aggressive emails. Veiled micro aggressions. Subtle, deliberate tests. It was a masterclass in controlled elitism.

I quickly realized I needed to shift gears. The same skillset I'd honed throughout life—code-switching, reading a room, mirroring energy before even stepping inside—became my most valuable asset.

Google prided itself on its DEI (Diversity, Equity, Inclusion) efforts. On the surface, it was progressive. Employee Resource Groups (ERGs) offered community and safe space—at least in theory. But even within these "inclusive" spaces, there were still quiet lines of exclusion.

Not long after joining, a member of the Black Googler Network (BGN) approached me to join. I didn't have to ask for acceptance—my Blackness got me through that door.

But there was another door I had hoped would open: the Asian-Pacific Islander (API) group. No one from that space ever reached out. No one ever recognized the Filipino part of me—the side just as real, just as lived.

Maybe it was how I looked. Maybe it was my energy. Maybe they just didn't see me as *one of them*. Whatever the reason, it reaffirmed what I had always known: I was visible and invisible at the same time. Seen, but never fully acknowledged. Still, I advanced.

I eventually became a DC chapter leader for the Black Googler Network. It was a position of privilege—and discomfort. On one hand, I was proud to sit at the table and advocate for Black equity within a corporate giant. On the other hand, I sometimes felt like a spectator in my own space.

The fireside chats. The panels. The guest speakers like Don Peebles. The conversations always centered on the *traditional* Black experience—pain, power, resilience. Stories I understood, but didn't always *embody*.

After one event, a guest approached me and said candidly: "It must be tough navigating these rooms with your background." He wasn't wrong.

Sometimes my ambiguity felt like a silent barrier. Not because I didn't experience the world as a Black man, but because in spaces where identity is defined by *shared* struggle, I didn't always feel like I had the right to fully claim it.

Still, I used my in-betweenness as a bridge.

Where others saw division, I saw opportunity.

I could move from the cooks in the Google kitchen to the SVP of Government Affairs without switching up who I was. My identity allowed me to flex—to shift between energies, dialects, experiences—with intention. I leaned into the ambiguity.

If I couldn't fully belong to one space, I could at least move between them with purpose. That ability became more than survival—it became *strategy*. And that, more than anything, shaped the way I built my career. I came to understand that my racial ambiguity wasn't just a trait. It was a tool, a currency, and at times, a shield.

It allowed me to move through doors that others had to fight to crack open. In a corporate landscape built on race, status, and power—I became a bridge.

The connections I fostered over time weren't just about networking or career advancement—they were about understanding people.

I learned how to translate the frustrations of lower-level employees into language executives would actually hear. I became the voice for those who felt they couldn't speak up—whether out of fear of retaliation or the belief that their concerns would be dismissed outright.

It wasn't lost on me that my ability to code-switch gave me an edge.

I don't care what stigma society tries to attach to it—code-switching isn't just about survival. It's strategy. When used intentionally, it becomes a privilege: a tool that helps you navigate conversations others wouldn't even get the chance to have. It allows you to articulate what others might overlook, break through bias, and redirect misunderstanding before it festers into conflict.

But with that privilege came responsibility.

As a leader, I made it my mission to show others that authentic leadership isn't about attention—it's about *impact*. It's about stepping up, even when no one's watching. Even when there's no immediate reward. If you have the power to influence, you have a duty to use it wisely.

My identity—a blend of cultures, experiences, and perspectives—opened doors I might never have entered otherwise. But once I was in the room, I had a choice:

Blend in quietly—or challenge the space to evolve.

I chose the latter.

OG MIKE

These days, I keep my circle small. Not because I'm antisocial, but because I've grown into a version of myself that values depth over breadth. I've learned the importance of being around people who see me *fully*—and that kind of connection doesn't come easy when you live in the in-between.

Racial ambiguity has followed me like a shadow—quiet, ever-present—in every introduction, every new space, every shifting friendship. I've been the "safe Black guy," the "not-really-Asian" friend, the one who could adapt to any group but never truly *belong* to one.

That made me a social chameleon—sharp, observant, quick to read a room, and easy to like. But the older I get, the more I realize: being liked is not the same as being known.

Today, I've curated relationships that allow me to bring *all* parts of myself to the table. No more performance. No more dimming who

I am to ease someone else's discomfort. But getting here wasn't easy.

It took years of trial and error. Friendships that taught me how people *perceive* me. Experiences that showed me how code-switching became instinct. And the sobering reality that trust doesn't come easy when people can't label you.

I'm still learning what it means to be fully *seen*, not just interpreted. And in that process, I've discovered that friendship—like identity—doesn't have to be defined by clarity. It can be shaped by connection, mutual respect, and the willingness to hold space for complexity.

It's the year 2025, and I've now lived half of my expected life span—a sobering milestone that demands reflection.

Standing at this midpoint, I find myself in a unique position—not just as a man straddling two racial identities, but as a millennial bridging two generational worldviews.

Growing up half-Black and half-Filipino in the '90s and early 2000s gave me what I still consider the best of both worlds. It was a time when technology enhanced, rather than consumed, our lives. When cultural exchange was accelerating—but hadn't yet been commodified. We witnessed the dawn of the internet, yet still knew the joy of playing outside, of learning from grandparents, of existing within *both* sides of a blended heritage.

But now, as adults, our generation faces challenges we never imagined as kids:

- A housing crisis
- Economic instability

- Climate anxiety
- And the relentless churn of identity politics, which seems to have calcified instead of evolved

GEN Z AND THE
WEIGHT OF PROGRESS

I often reflect on my parents' journey—a Black father and Filipino mother who fell in love during a time when anti-miscegenation sentiments still lingered in many communities.

Their courage, the barriers they broke, and the prejudice they endured make some of my own struggles feel . . . small by comparison. Their generation faced fire hoses, exclusionary laws, and institutional silence. They fought for representation. They *changed* the system from the outside.

While my generation tweets about micro aggressions, theirs faced down police dogs.

There's a humbling contrast in that.

What surprises me most today is my reaction to Gen Z—their seemingly effortless embrace of multiculturalism. I meet twenty-somethings who've grown up in such diverse environments that they seem almost *colorblind*. Not in the dismissive sense, but in a way that genuinely doesn't understand *why* racial differences would cause division in the first place.

Their natural ease with mixed identities like mine should feel like validation.

And yet . . . sometimes it leaves me feeling displaced. Because the very struggle that shaped me—the constant explaining, adapting, defining—feels like it's becoming irrelevant.

Is this progress? Undoubtedly. But there's a complexity here that I can't ignore.

When younger peers miss the historical context in conversations about race, or when they fail to recognize coded bias, I wonder if we're witnessing evolution . . . or erasure.

My experience—of being "too Black" in one room and "too Asian" in another—gave me a cultural literacy rooted in survival. It taught me how to decode energy, read silence, and understand what *wasn't* being said.

That fluency—of navigating the unsaid—feels increasingly rare.

And I wonder: What happens when that language disappears?

This awareness has made me more selective about my social engagements. The performative aspects of today's "PC culture" exhaust me—not because I oppose respectful language or inclusivity, but because surface-level language policing often replaces genuine understanding.

I treasure those rare friendships where we can speak honestly about race, culture, and identity without the constant fear of inadvertent offense or misinterpretation. These conversations aren't about clinging to outdated prejudices—they're about acknowledging the messiness of human experience and the imperfect ways we categorize ourselves and others.

My racial journey has taught me to live in that difficult space between tradition and progress. I respect my Filipino grandmother's cultural conservatism, while also recognizing which values need to evolve. I honor Black cultural traditions, while questioning the elements that may no longer serve our collective good.

This ability to hold seemingly contradictory positions at once is, perhaps, the greatest gift of my mixed heritage. I learned early on that binary thinking rarely captures the fullness of human identity.

THE FACE-TO-FACE ERA VERSUS THE CURATED SELF

Social media has profoundly altered how we form and express identity.

Where I once had to navigate physical spaces—friend gatherings where my melanin and fine hair marked me as different, or Black community events where my Asian features raised questions—today's youth construct their identities through carefully curated online personas.

The authenticity I was forced to develop through face-to-face confrontations with differences seems increasingly rare in a world where people can simply block, mute, or unfollow any perspective that challenges them.

Those uncomfortable moments—standing in rooms where I didn't quite fit, feeling the weight of stares that questioned my belonging—weren't just challenges to overcome; they were *formative*. They built the resilience I carry today. The social anxiety I once felt walking into unfamiliar spaces sharpened my understanding of human behavior and cultural nuance.

In contrast, today's digital interactions—with their safety nets of distance and anonymity—rarely demand the same level of emotional intelligence or adaptability.

My relationships have evolved with this awareness.

Gone are the days when I played the perpetual bridge between communities, exhausting myself trying to translate experiences across cultural divides. I've learned that healthy boundaries aren't a form of selfishness—they're *self-preservation*.

After years of contorting myself—being "more Black" in some rooms, "more Filipino" in others—I've embraced independence from external definitions.

FAITH AS INTEGRATION

What surprises me most is how this journey has led me to faith.

> *"Come near to God and He will come near to you."*
> **James 4:8**

It's never cliché to find God after suffering—especially when that suffering comes from decades of navigating spaces where you never quite fit.

I learned that He meets you where you are.

Because it's all about His timing—a divine patience I've come to appreciate as someone who has spent a lifetime explaining his existence at the intersection of Black and Filipino identity.

I didn't find the Savior until 2023.

It wasn't that I didn't believe in The Lord and Savior, Jesus Christ, but I didn't have a real relationship with Him.

Much like my early approach to race, I acknowledged the facts without embracing the deeper connection. I existed in the borderlands of faith—just as I had existed in the borderlands of race. Present, but unanchored.

Finding a nondenominational church community in my thirties wasn't something I expected, but it offered a framework for integration I didn't realize I needed.

There's something profoundly healing about a space that emphasizes our shared humanity while still honoring our differences.

My spirituality hasn't erased the complexities of my racial identity, but it has helped me place them in a larger context.

This isn't to say I've become some model of religious virtue—far from it. I still wrestle with the same questions of belonging and identity that have followed me since childhood.

But now, I approach those questions from a place of humility instead of defensiveness. And that shift has opened new pathways for connection and growth.

My mixed heritage taught me early that rigid categories rarely capture the totality of human experience. My faith has simply extended that understanding to encompass the spiritual dimension as well.

Standing at this midpoint in life, I find myself less concerned with which box I check on demographic forms and more focused on the quality of my connections—with family, with community, and with something larger than myself.

The racial ambiguity that once felt like a burden has become a lens through which I see past surface differences to deeper commonalities.

In a world increasingly fragmented by identity politics, maybe this perspective—of nuance, of empathy, of lived contradiction—is exactly what we need.

> *"If you belonged to the world, it would love you as its own. As it is, you do not belong to the world, but I have chosen you out of the world."*
> **John 15:19**

AN INCOMPLETE SANCTUARY

We didn't go to church regularly as a family. We didn't pray together, either.

This sporadic spirituality mirrored how we approached race—discussed only when necessary, avoided when uncomfortable.

I wonder if my father's distance from organized religion stemmed from how Black churches often reinforced the same community boundaries my mixed identity challenged.

I was told he had been deeply involved in church growing up. Maybe he burned out. Or maybe he realized that even sacred spaces offered incomplete sanctuary for a man raising biracial children in a world obsessed with categorization.

My mother was like most Filipinos: Catholic, though she regularly attended a Protestant church on Fort Meade. Her religious hybridity—raised in Catholic tradition but practicing Protestant faith—paralleled my own experience of cultural hybridity. My brother and I would accompany her at least once a month, mostly because afterward, we got to go to Burba Lake and play at the park.

Even in childhood, church felt like another performance space—another room where I had to present a version of myself that met someone else's expectations. Sit still. Stay quiet. Follow along. Don't ask uncomfortable questions about why Jesus in the stained glass looked nothing like me, or like either side of my family.

I never really got into Catholicism. I didn't understand what they were saying. The Latin phrases and ritualistic movements felt just as foreign as the Tagalog spoken by my Filipino relatives. The only connection I had to God at the time was through tithing and communion—physical acts that didn't require explanation or acknowledgment of my complex identity. Beyond that, no one taught me how to read the Bible or how important spiritual life could be—just as no one taught me how to read the subtle cues in a room to figure out which part of my racial identity to amplify or minimize.

Later, as a teenager, my brother and I weren't allowed to spend the night at friends' houses unless we agreed to attend church with them the next morning. That conditional freedom mirrored the conditional acceptance I often felt in monoracial spaces. You can be here—but understand, the rules are different for you. So we returned to church, this time a Baptist one. But the results were similar. I wasn't drawn to the long sermons or the singing. Just being there felt like enough—another version of a skill I had mastered early: showing up physically while never fully belonging.

Even so, it felt good to be told I was "saved." Even back then, I knew I had habits that weren't the best, and I feared I might go to hell. That fear of eternal judgment sometimes felt like a metaphor for the racial judgment I lived with daily—being evaluated, being watched, being labeled by standards I never fully understood or agreed to.

Despite my lack of spiritual grounding, I always had a belief in a higher purpose—an internal compass that kept me in check. My mixed heritage gave me that foundation, even when I didn't know what to call it. I believed there was meaning to my perspective, even when I couldn't yet articulate it.

It may have been a blessing that I wasn't fully immersed in religion during those years. If I had been, I might've steered clear of some of the questionable decisions I later made. Like many mixed-race individuals, I sometimes sought belonging in spaces that didn't truly value me. I made choices based on whichever version of myself felt more accepted in that moment. My spiritual journey, much like my racial one, has been about authenticity over acceptance—about discovering that true belonging doesn't come from squeezing into boxes, but from learning to live fully in my complexity.

There's also grief attached to all of this. My brother wasn't a church person either, and with his passing, I sometimes wonder if he made it to God's Kingdom. That question lingers heavy on my heart. It mirrors other forms of loss—like the Filipino customs my kids may never know, or the Black cultural wisdom that gets more diluted with each generation. Whether in faith or culture, what we fail to pass down risks being lost. And that accumulation of loss becomes a deeper kind of grief.

When I reconnected with God in 2023, it wasn't just about

salvation. It was about finding a structure that could hold all the contradictions—the fragments of identity that never seemed to fit together in the world's neat little categories. My faith didn't erase the complexity of being Black and Filipino. It gave me a place to hold it.

Growing up with trauma—healed or not—was a common thread in my generation. We raised ourselves and often mistook dysfunction and abuse for normalcy. For someone like me, straddling two racial identities, that self-raising came with an added layer of complexity: navigating cultural expectations that often contradicted each other. I had to learn which parts of myself to reveal and which to withhold, depending on the space I was in. I became fluent in reading rooms, sensing whether my presence would be embraced or questioned. That constant hyperawareness wasn't just born from being a millennial—it was a survival mechanism sharpened by the challenge of being racially ambiguous in a world that demands definition.

I watched how friends manipulated women, how instigators pushed others into reckless decisions. I saw it all through a lens shaped by dual cultures—how those same behaviors played out differently in Black spaces than in Filipino gatherings. The machismo in Filipino households mirrored, yet diverged from, the expressions of masculinity I saw in Black communities. I had no singular blueprint for manhood. Instead, I was left to piece together my own version, drawing from examples that often conflicted more than they aligned. My mixed heritage gave me just enough distance to notice the patterns—but not enough to escape their influence.

What I needed—though I didn't know it then—was healing. Healing from the social pressure I had quietly accumulated over the years. From constantly having to explain my existence. From the patient, smiling responses to "What are you?" that masked the exhaustion. From code-switching so seamlessly that I sometimes forgot which version of myself was the most real. The stress of that identity juggling didn't scream. It simmered, slowly draining me.

That healing began when I hit rock bottom.

I was in the middle of a failing relationship with my long-term girlfriend—the mother of my child. We had weathered the storm of introducing each other to our families, navigating cultural expectations, unspoken rules, and the awkward tension that came with mixing two lineages in one household. We tried, but we were unraveling.

Then came the layoff. I lost my job, and after the breakup, I had no choice but to move back in with my parents. I couldn't afford a place of my own. Returning home meant walking back into a space that bore every reminder of who I was and who I had been. Soul food sat next to lumpia on the dinner table. Our family photo albums were full of blended skin tones and tangled lineages—a visible reminder of everything I embodied and still struggled to define.

And while all this unfolded, I was deep in a child custody battle—fighting for full custody of my first son. The court system, with its checkboxes and assumptions, wasn't built for men like me. The forms never made space for nuance. I was asked to select a race, as if one word could carry the weight of my ancestry. Lawyers made assumptions based on how I looked. I thought about my son—what boxes would he check one day? What questions would he be asked that I still didn't have answers for?

My life had fallen apart, and I had no blueprint for how to rebuild it.

The identity that once helped me blend into spaces, to adapt and translate, now felt flimsy and insufficient. I turned to prayer—not the rehearsed recitations from childhood, not the call-and-response praise from Black churches, but something raw. A private surrender. A reaching out from that place between all things, where I had always lived.

I started watching church services online—letting the messages settle in the silence of my room. I fasted from social media, stepping away from the endless cycle of image curation and identity performance. I gave up smoking weed, realizing I no longer wanted escape. I wanted clarity. I needed transformation, not just survival.

I was ready to begin again. To build a life where my racial ambiguity wasn't a burden to bear but a perspective to honor. A life that embraced the full spectrum of who I was—not just to prove something to the world, but to finally feel whole within myself.

> *"Do not conform to the pattern of this world, but be transformed by the renewing of your mind."*
> **Romans 12:2**

I had begun to feel like my relationships meant nothing—because no matter how much I poured into others, I rarely received the same fulfillment in return. That imbalance wasn't just emotional; it was rooted in the deeper dynamic of always being the bridge—the one who could connect others, translate cultures, make people feel seen. But in the midst of rebuilding my life, I found myself growing more solitary, questioning everything I thought I knew about myself. I was the man who had spent a lifetime adapting to the expectations of others. Now I had to ask: Who was I when no one was watching?

It wasn't until a girl I knew started consistently posting about Union Church that something shifted. Her videos were full of energy, joy, and a kind of engagement I hadn't seen in church spaces before. Something stirred in me, telling me to go. As it often happens, this moment aligned with Easter weekend—a holiday I had always observed out of cultural habit, not spiritual conviction. Still, it felt like the right time. I decided to attend Union Church at the BWI campus, led by Pastor Stephen Chandler.

Though it was a nondenominational church, the strong presence of Black congregants made it feel reminiscent of a Methodist community. And once again, I wondered how I would be perceived. Would I be seen as Black enough? Would I be questioned, silently or otherwise, about my identity—my appearance, my ancestry, my right to belong? But I went, and I remember that first sermon vividly. Pastor Chandler spoke about the Holy Trinity—Flesh, Soul, and Spirit—and how it reflected our lives.

It hit me in a way I didn't expect.

I shouldn't have been surprised. I've always had to shift depending on the room—father, partner, son, leader. And on top of those roles, I've had to hold my racial identity the same way: I'm Black, I'm Filipino—but I'm both, at the same time. That day, the message gave me language I hadn't had before.

"Just as a body, though one, has many parts, but all its many parts form one body, so it is with Christ."
1 Corinthians 12:12

That verse struck something deep within me. I had never thought to apply my life in a biblical context before. But here it was—a spiritual framework that didn't ask me to separate or choose between my identities. Instead, it affirmed the idea that unity can be made of many parts. Multiplicity wasn't a flaw. It was part of a divine design.

The number 2, I later learned, holds powerful significance in the Bible: separation and diversity, partnership and balance. That resonated with me. My life had always reflected duality—Black and Filipino, not in opposition but in harmony. Where I had once seen contradiction, I now saw completeness. My in-between identity was no longer something to defend or explain; it was something to embrace.

That realization pulled me deeper into the faith. Week after week, I found myself needing church—not just as a tradition but as a lifeline. Sunday became sacred. The environment was unlike anything I'd known growing up. It was vibrant, engaging, and the message of God was delivered in a way that felt real, relevant, and approachable. And more than that, the congregation looked like the world I lived in—diverse, imperfect, seeking something greater.

Some Sundays, I found myself in tears. Not because of sadness exactly, but because something would rise to the surface—an emotional burden long buried—and I'd feel a deep need to let it go. I cried for all the different versions of myself I'd carried. For the child who realized early on that he didn't fully look like either side of his family. For the teen who prepared answers to questions like: "What are you?" before they were even asked. For the adult who often felt both hyper visible and unseen, depending on the space.

Eventually, I came to understand the missing piece in my life wasn't friendships, or romantic relationships, or even a sense of success. I was missing the love of Jesus. And with that came a deeper understanding—that God, our Father, didn't make mistakes. He created me with intention. I was born to be different. Cut from a different cloth.

> *"For you created my inmost being; you knit me together in my mother's womb. I praise you because I am fearfully and wonderfully made; your works are wonderful, I know that full well."*
> **Psalm 139:13–14**

In faith, I discovered a narrative that reframed my racial ambiguity—not as a social inconvenience, but as divine intention. The world I had spent so long trying to fit into was never designed for easy acceptance. Just as they denied Jesus and later crucified Him for being a prophet they couldn't comprehend, I, too, had felt the sting of rejection for simply existing in a space that challenged people's categories.

This spiritual revelation transformed how I viewed my racial journey. What if the very thing that had caused me so much internal conflict—existing between classifications in a world obsessed with labels—was actually my greatest strength? What if my ability to see through multiple lenses, to navigate and bridge different worlds, wasn't incidental but essential to my purpose?

In Christ's story—misunderstood, doubted, and ultimately rejected by those who could not grasp His nature—I found deep resonance. I had spent my life being questioned, asked to explain who I was, expected to simplify what was never simple. And now, for the first time, I saw my mixed heritage not as a burden to carry but as a gift with purpose. It gave me a unique perspective—one that could understand division and still see the possibility of unity.

"Before I formed you in the womb I knew you, before you were born I set you apart; I appointed you as a prophet to the nations."
Jeremiah 1:5

My journey through racial ambiguity had unknowingly prepared me for a faith that transcends boxes and binaries—a faith that sees God not in the limits of identity but in the sacredness of the space in between.

GENERATIONAL MIDDLE CHILD

"I want my hair to look like yours," my son said one morning as we stood in the mirror together. He said it casually, like it was just about style. But I knew better. That sentence carried history, identity, and hope. It reminded me how much of my life has been spent translating what others never thought to explain.

My son's hair is soft and loosely curled. Mine is straight and silky. Not better. Not worse. Just different. Yet even at his young age, he was already picking up on the world's quiet signals—the unspoken hierarchy placed on texture, shade, and features. It wasn't that he had "bad hair." It was that society has conditioned us to believe straight is normal, loose curls are acceptable, and anything "too Black" is somehow too much.

I didn't teach him that. But the world did. Now it's up to me to teach him something else.

That's when I understood: being a father, a son, and a cultural bridge means you're always translating.

I've always been a translator.

Not just between languages—though I've done that too—but between worlds. Between my Black father and my Filipino mother. Between relatives who didn't share the same words, and sometimes, not even the same emotional language.

As I've gotten older, I realize I'm also translating across generations—between the analog grit of Gen X, the adaptable hustle of millennials like myself, and the fluid, digital fluency of Gen Z. Each generation speaks its own dialect of identity, resilience, and love.

Gen X, like my parents, kept their emotions close. They believed in showing love through sacrifice and duty, not declarations. They didn't air their business, and pain was something you dealt with privately. My generation—the millennials—were the first to start naming our trauma, to try therapy, to turn vulnerability into vocabulary. And Gen Z? They grew up with emotional language baked into their culture. They were raised with Wi-Fi and smartphones, and with that came a fluency that can sometimes feel foreign, even though I'm just one step ahead.

When I talk to my son or my younger cousins, I'm not just translating culture. I'm translating eras.

I explain why Grandpa doesn't express emotion easily. Why Lola says, "you gained weight," like it's a compliment. Why the word "ambiguous," even when meant kindly, can still make me flinch. These are the things we don't always teach directly—but they shape us. And if we don't bridge the gaps, that meaning is lost.

Cultural inheritance isn't just about recipes or holidays. It's about context.

It's about explaining not just *what* was done, but *why*—and when it might be time to let certain things evolve. I often find myself defending the past to the future, and explaining the future to the past. And truthfully, it's exhausting.

But it's also sacred work.

I used to resent being in the middle—between races, between expectations, between generations. Now, I see it as purpose. Not everyone is built to be a bridge. But maybe I was.

Translation doesn't just happen across generations—it happens within us, too. Especially in families like mine, where expectations are strong but explanations are rare. Their love was real, but not always verbal. So I learned to translate tone, body language, and the unspoken rules between the lines.

Expectations were everywhere, layered under every interaction. Be respectful—but not too opinionated. Be successful—but don't forget where you come from. Carry both cultures with pride—but don't question the parts that don't make sense. I was navigating a map without a legend, trying to translate two cultures and two generations into a language I could live by.

And the thing is—none of that translation was visible. To the outside world, I just looked like I was adapting. But on the inside, I was constantly calculating:

Which version of me do I need to be right now? Who do I disappoint less by choosing this path? What do I risk by being fully myself? Some of that pressure still lingers.

When I discipline my son, I hear my father's voice in my tone. But I also pause and ask—am I parenting from tradition or from healing?

When my mom gives me advice, I know it's out of love. But it's also rooted in a worldview built on survival, not emotional freedom. I feel her worry when I step away from the "safe" path—even though, for someone like me, safety has never been guaranteed.

Internal translation is exhausting. But it's also sacred. It's how we honor those who raised us without becoming carbon copies of their choices. It's how we move the story forward without erasing where it began.

I remember growing up, I couldn't question my dad's authority—even when I knew in my gut something didn't feel right. I'd be full of emotion, words rising like a tide I wasn't allowed to release. His word was final. Not to be challenged. Not to be unpacked. That silence became its own kind of inheritance—passed down not out of malice, but out of necessity. He was raising me the way he had been raised: to follow the rules, to respect the chain of command, to fall in line even when it hurt.

One memory that sticks with me is asking—again and again—if I could spend the night at my best friend's house. I already knew how it would go:

"Ask your mother." "Ask your father." Back and forth, like a game with no winner.

It felt unfair, especially because my best friend was white—and his household ran by a completely different playbook. He had freedom. Resources. Room to explore. I felt caged by what I didn't yet understand: that my parents weren't just saying, "no." They were protecting something. Preserving the values of two cultures. Trying to make sure I didn't get swallowed up by someone else's norm.

Now, as a father, I feel those moments echo in my own decisions. When my son asks why he can't do something, I don't shut him down with a cold "because I said so." I've learned the power of explanation—of having thoughtful conversations. Not because I owe him a debate, but because I want him to feel heard. I want him to know that emotion isn't weakness. That discipline doesn't require silence. That correction doesn't have to strip away dignity.

The older he gets, the more I try to prepare him for the world—not by hardening him, but by equipping him. I teach him to hold both expectation and reality. To know when to comply, and when to ask why. These were lessons I learned the long way—through missteps, silence, and slowly building inner trust.

Raising a daughter brings its own kind of translation. I never had a sister, so most of what I knew about girls came from short visits to my cousins' houses. But nothing prepares you for being the father of a little girl who sees you as her first love. My daughter isn't just sweet and strong—she's curious, confident, and constantly questioning the world. One day, she'll face some of the same unspoken pressures I did—being judged before she's known, being asked to explain herself before she can just *be*.

So, I try to balance my approach. I keep them close to the environments I grew up in—not to limit them, but to root them. I surround them with diversity. I give them experiences I only dreamed of. Because if I'm the bridge, then they're the crossing. And it's my responsibility to make sure what they walk across is strong, honest, and wide enough to hold everything they're becoming.

In honoring our dual identity—Black and Filipino—I make it a point to take my kids to every major holiday at my aunt's house. It's more than just a meal. It's tradition. It's memory. It's the blend of everything I was raised on, wrapped into one day. The smell of lumpia frying in the kitchen, the warmth of chicken adobo simmering on the stove, sharing a table with collard greens and baked mac and cheese. That table tells a story. One of survival, of culture, of legacy.

My kids run around the same backyard I once did, playing with my cousins' children—the next generation already bonding over soda spills, video games, and shared laughter. And for a few hours, it feels like nothing has changed. The voices of my childhood echo through the walls, now layered with new ones. We tell old stories, roast each other the way only family can, and our kids soak it all in—probably not realizing that these are the moments that will shape them. That this is what home feels like—even if it only happens a few times a year.

Outside of holidays, I make sure we explore other cultures, too. Sometimes we'll hit a Korean BBQ spot. Other times we'll stroll through an Asian food festival, trying takoyaki or bao buns under a canopy of paper lanterns. But most often, home is wherever the kitchen is. Just like my mom did for me, I cook for my kids. It's an unspoken language of love. There's always something ready—a big breakfast with spam and eggs, sandwiches packed for lunch, or a simple steak dinner. Nothing extravagant, but always intentional.

Nourishment as tradition. Food as translation.

And then there's music.

I realized one day that the songs my kids are growing up with don't mark time the same way they did for me. There's something different about today's sound—less memory, more moment. So, I fill the house with old-school music. Marvin, Prince, The Gap Band. I play them while I'm cleaning, lounging, or just trying to keep the energy grounded. It feels like I'm lacing the air with memory, threading my own nostalgia into their everyday lives.

One of my favorite moments was watching my daughter dance to Michael Jackson for the first time. I had pulled up the *Smooth Criminal* short film and sat her down, saying, "Watch this . . . this was magic to us." Her eyes lit up. She mimicked his moves the best she could—spinning, sliding, clapping out of rhythm but full of joy. She didn't fully understand it yet, but I could see the wonder building in her.

That's what matters most to me: giving them pieces of the past that still live, still breathe. I'm not trying to trap them in nostalgia. I'm giving them anchors—cultural and emotional bookmarks they can revisit. So maybe one day, they'll play that same music for their own kids. And maybe they'll remember how their dad made a house feel like history and future at the same time.

Being a millennial often feels like standing at the midpoint of a cultural bridge—one foot rooted in analog memory, the other stepping cautiously into digital inheritance. I grew up in a world where you had to memorize phone numbers, where you got yelled at for tying up the house phone, and where the internet screamed at you through dial-up before finally letting you log onto AIM. Now I'm raising kids in a world where FaceTime is second nature and their first instinct is to Google what they don't know.

Millennials like me—we were raised by Gen Xers and are now raising Gen Z. That gives us a double lens. We watched the world shift under our feet—from VHS to streaming, from handwritten notes to TikTok videos, from encyclopedias to Wikipedia. And we still remember what it was like to be in a moment without needing to document it.

Public opinion about Gen Z is often divided—some praise them as the most inclusive and outspoken generation; others criticize them for being overly sensitive and glued to their screens. But what's undeniable is their power. Gen Z has a collective confidence that disrupts systems, questions tradition, and forces institutions to change. They've turned social media from a pastime into a platform. What we millennials used to whisper in safe spaces, Gen Z says out loud, on record, and in real time.

Where we were shaped by the birth of the internet, they were born inside it. That difference matters. It shapes how they understand truth, build relationships, and define success. They're quick to cancel—but also quick to organize. They'll call out injustice in a meme and start a movement with a hashtag. Their urgency sometimes clashes with our patience—but that friction is where transformation happens.

One moment that crystallized the generational and cultural shift for me was during the injustice surrounding Trayvon Martin. I was working in the heart of Baltimore, watching the headlines unfold during George Zimmerman's trial. Social media turned that trial from another news cycle into a synchronized cry. It wasn't just about a hoodie or a pack of Skittles—it was about identity, profiling, and the terrifying truth that a Black child could be deemed a threat just for existing. For many of us, it was the first time social platforms gave us a collective voice. A digital uprising.

Baltimore was tense. The National Guard rolled in like it was wartime—tanks on city blocks, soldiers on corners, rifles slung with purpose. The air was thick with distrust. Not just in Zimmerman's acquittal, but in the system itself. As a Black father, watching the story of another Black boy judged and lost—there was no distance between their grief and my own. I carried it. I still do.

And yet, when the Stop Asian Hate movement began gaining momentum, I felt . . . .separate. Like I should have felt more connected—but didn't. I watched people with even the faintest thread of Asian ancestry step forward, make their voices known. And while I understood the urgency, the emotion didn't land the same way for me.

Maybe it's because, growing up, I didn't see Asian identity under attack in the same way Black identity always had been. Or maybe it's because that side of my heritage hadn't fully embraced me. I'd spent a lifetime living in the in-between, and this was just another reminder of how isolating that space can be.

Even in the workplace—where DEI conversations were finally evolving from checkbox exercises to genuine calls for change—I could feel the shift. After George Floyd's murder, colleagues checked in on me. There were quiet conversations, visible tears, and "safe spaces" created almost overnight. But when headlines turned to attacks against Asians, the silence was deafening. No one asked how I was feeling—not even those who knew my background. It was as if that part of me had disappeared from the narrative altogether.

I often attribute that disconnect to the isolating effects of COVID-19. For over a year, we lived in silos, distanced from each other and immersed in our own echo chambers. We were left alone with our thoughts—and whatever narratives the media chose to amplify. Maybe that's why the solidarity didn't last. Maybe that's why the grief felt by the Asian community never fully resonated with me. The movement lost momentum, and for people like myself, caught between identities, that absence was more than noticeable—it was personal.

This is the paradox of being mixed in a world that still prefers its identities to be binary. Being a millennial caught between analog empathy and digital outrage. We have the language now. The platforms. The hashtags. But the nuance—the full truth of who gets embraced, who gets left out, and who's asked to translate it all—is still catching up.

Over time, I developed a kind of distance from being politically outspoken—not because I didn't care, but as a defense against the noise. I chose to speak through truths and facts, rather than get tangled in the web of opinions and assumptions. But during Trump's second campaign cycle, it became harder to ignore the temperature of the country. The MAGA flags. The dog whistles are buried beneath "good old boy" nostalgia. The storming of the Capitol—an act that, had the rioters been Black, would've ended in bloodshed.

It was another rupture. Another reminder of how fragile American ideals become when Black bodies are at the center of the story. That election, like those before it, made clear that political affiliation wasn't just about policy—it was about values, about identity, about which lives were deemed worthy of protection.

And then came Kamala Harris.

The first Black woman to be nominated for vice president—a moment that should have been universally celebrated, but wasn't. I watched as public opinion pulled her apart. Her Blackness was dissected. Her Indian heritage scrutinized. Her ambition labeled as opportunistic. People questioned her roots, her accent, even her playlist. The very qualities that should have connected her to multiple communities somehow became liabilities.

Maybe that's what hurt the most—watching someone who looked like me, who carried many of the same intersections, be questioned simply for existing in a space we were always told to aspire to.

There was this unspoken expectation that she needed to be all things to all people—an expectation I know too well. To be "Black enough" when it benefits the community. To be "other" when it suits the room. Kamala's Howard degree gave her HBCU credibility, but her upbringing and career didn't always align with a singular cultural script. And Gen Z—armed with edits, captions, and curated outrage—had no hesitation holding her accountable, even as older generations celebrated her as a symbol of progress.

It became a generational tension: one side fighting for legacy, the other for clarity.

In the swirl of posts, memes, and hot takes, I found myself in quiet shock—not just at the volume of voices, but at how personal it all felt. Because I, too, have lived in spaces where the narrative sometimes fits, and other times doesn't. Where identity is parsed and policed by people who haven't walked your path, and while I believe in accountability, I also believe in grace.

I wouldn't want to pass judgment on someone trying to lead through the noise, just because they haven't yet figured out how to articulate all of it. That, too, is part of the in-between. The bridge between analog and digital. Between gut and algorithm. Between representation and reality.

Beyond the headlines and history-making elections, cultural translation happens in the everyday. In the seemingly small choices that shape how I absorb the world around me. It's not just about identity in a political sense—it's about the images and stories I let

MICHAEL GOODLOE

in, the music I play, the books I read, and how I interpret each one through a layered lens not everyone carries.

DEI AS HUMANITY'S SOUL

My biased opinion strongly suggests that life inherently requires diversity. Often, people are asked to define what diversity, equity, and inclusion mean to them—seemingly a simple question, yet challenging to articulate unless you've lived through marginalization or genuinely experienced diverse environments. For me, growing up racially ambiguous—half Black and half Filipino—this question holds a more intimate complexity. It's not just about representation; it's about belonging in spaces where you're never quite sure who fully sees you.

DEI, to me, means thriving in communities where people don't always look like you, and where even those who do might still question your legitimacy. It means challenging norms that demand neat boxes, and instead providing access across the board while intentionally inviting all shades of identity to the table. It's not just a doctrine of words in our constitution or mission statements, but a moral responsibility—a compass that should guide us as we move through life with integrity and compassion.

As someone who has often felt both seen and unseen—too Black for some circles, not Black enough for others, and almost invisible within the Asian community—I've come to understand that inclusion is not a passive idea. It's active work. True diversity isn't simply achieved through optics or buzzwords. It exists in daily acts: acknowledging the unspoken, hearing the unheard, and making space where none existed before.

Some of the most brilliant minds have joined forces across cultural, religious, and ideological lines to build the groundwork for a more just society. But that same society still wrestles with the lingering ghosts of past ideologies—those rooted in the "good ol' boy" systems, quietly perpetuating separate-but-equal mindsets. Being racially ambiguous means you're often the litmus test for how far society has truly come. You're the conversation starter, the contradiction in the room, the living reminder that identity is layered.

DEI shouldn't be reduced to a corporate initiative or a one-off workshop. For people like me, it's not theoretical—it's lived. It's in the questions I'm asked, the assumptions people make, the spaces I enter where I'm expected to decode my presence. I would self-nominate as a subject matter expert on the nuances of identity because my life has required me to be. I've had to adapt, navigate, and sometimes educate—often all at once.

To me, diversity, equity, and inclusion are not optional frameworks; they are essential truths. They are the soul of our humanity, and the bridge between understanding and othering. And every time we choose to see someone fully—in all their complexity—we take a step closer to the world we claim to want. That's the version of DEI I believe in. The one that makes space for stories like mine.

THE BLASIAN ABSENCE IN POP CULTURE

When I watch a film, I'm not just following the protagonist's journey—I'm scanning for who's missing. I notice the stereotypes others might dismiss as harmless. I pick up on coded language, on casting choices, on cultural nuances that hit differently depending on which side of my heritage I'm leaning into that day.

Watching *The Wood* brought me back to a space that felt both familiar and affirming—a coming-of-age story rooted in Blackness, but filled with tenderness, vulnerability, and a sense of place that mirrored how many of us came into ourselves. It wasn't about trauma or survival. It was about the ordinary: school dances, first crushes, brotherhood, and the little rites of passage that shaped who we became.

Still, I found myself wondering where stories like mine—stories of in-betweenness, of being Black and something else—might exist on screen. There was pride in watching it, but also a quiet ache for the fuller story that still hasn't been told.

Sure, there were Black characters. There were Asian characters. But there were few—if any—that looked like me, sounded like me, or carried the dual weight of being both.

Representation wasn't just scarce. It was nonexistent.

I was a Blasian kid in the '90s and 2000s, flipping through channels, hoping to find some mirror that reflected who I was. But television and movies gave me fragments. I saw parts of myself in Will Smith's confidence, in Jet Li's discipline, in Omar Epps's cool. But none of them had a Filipino mother and a Black father. None of them had to answer, "What are you?" every time they walked into a new room.

The only biracial men that occasionally surfaced in mainstream media were often Black and white. And even then, their mixed identity was either completely ignored or flattened into whatever was more convenient for the story. Tiger Woods was one of the earliest public figures I could point to and say, "He's kind of like me." But even he coined the term "Cablinasian" and was rarely embraced fully by any one community.

When I looked for Blasian representation, I was met with silence.

There were no leading men in movies or sitcoms who looked like me. No pop stars navigating two distinct cultural lineages. No athletes or actors who openly discussed what it meant to live in the liminal space between Blackness and Asianness. The times that I saw representation, the character was downplayed and made to look weak. I remember watching *The Brothers*, a classic black film of four African-American men take on love, sex, and friendship—an exploration of the battle between the sexes. There was a particular scene that places the guys in a club after Jackson, played by Morris Chestnut takes a break from Denise, as Gabrielle Union, to go back out and explore the dating scene. To Jackson's disliking, Denise is in the club walking with another man on her arm who is portrayed as a bi-racial man named Cee-No, played by Henry Kingi Jr., who is an Black and Japanese descent. In that scene, Jackson quickly sizes up the competition and states, "he's not her type."

Bill Bellamy, a hilarious comic that he is, replies with, "is he white?" and follows DL Hughley, interjecting with: "Nah, Nah, Nah, I think he's Asian."

The questioning continues to fit him in a box with another funny remark from Bill Bellamy: "Maybe he's Latino or one of them Indians."

Scenarios like this would play in my head about how other men perceived me in a world that felt the need to label me.

That absence wasn't just about visibility. It affected how I saw myself. If you're never reflected, you begin to feel like a glitch. Like you're somehow off-script. It reinforces the idea that your experience is too niche, too complicated, too "other" to be part of the mainstream narrative.

Even in music, there's translation happening. I grew up on soul, deep house music, and hip-hop, but also on the love ballads my mom played while cleaning—Whitney Houston, Boyz II Men, and the occasional kundiman-style love song from her CD collection. I could jump between Tupac and Luther Vandross or Robin Stone, depending on the room I was in.

But today, when I hear rap filtered through Gen Z's lens—more melodic, more genre-blending—I sometimes feel like a translator between what was and what is. I find myself explaining to my kids why a Tupac lyric hits harder than a viral TikTok track—not just out of nostalgia, but because of context. That song came from lived experience. It was protest in rhyme.

And then there was Heavy D—smooth, charismatic, and unapologetically open about his attraction to women of all shades. He brought a kind of joyful inclusivity to his music that felt affirming for someone like me, living in multiple cultural spaces. His videos featured women of all races, and it didn't feel performative—it felt honest. It reflected his world and his taste.

That kind of multicultural appreciation rarely crosses into other genres. In rock, for example, women of color are often missing or flattened into stereotypes. There's rarely a celebration of diversity, rarely a sense that attraction can cross racial lines without commentary. That absence feels loud when you've seen it done right elsewhere.

In the early '70s and '80s, music carried a depth of soul and vulnerability that transcended identity. It was a time when men could express heartbreak, yearning, and intimacy without it being labeled as weakness. Artists poured their truths into ballads and grooves, creating a kind of euphoria that resonated—even if their faces didn't match the emotions in their lyrics.

I remember vibing to Color Me Badd, how their harmonies hit like a classic R&B group—only to later learn the lead singer was white. It was jarring, but not in a bad way. It mirrored real life: voices and identities rarely line up in neat boxes.

Even the recent revival of music like "yacht rock"—that smooth blend of jazz chords, soul, and subtle funk—reminds me of how fluid music can be when we stop trying to confine it. That genre, intentionally or not, bridged race and class because of how it felt—not how it looked.

Back then, part of the magic was mystery. You didn't know everything about an artist. There was no scrolling through social media to learn who they dated or what they believed. The voice was the entry point, not the persona.

I was nearly thirty when I learned Bobby Caldwell was white. It didn't change how his music made me feel. If anything, it deepened my reflection—how pure the connection had been before context colored it. His tone carried the warmth and weight of a Motown legend. That's what drew me in.

It's like the early stages of a relationship—when a voice over the phone creates a whole image in your mind before you ever see the face. Shows like *Love Is Blind* are built on that premise: emotional resonance before appearance.

And maybe that's what we're missing now—space for male artists, especially men of color, to be complex, mysterious, even soft. Vulnerability didn't always come wrapped in pain or trauma. Sometimes, it was smooth, sweet, soulful.

Fast forward to today, and Drake stands as one of the most recognizable figures in modern music—not just for his chart-toppers, but for the complicated mirror he holds up to identity. As a biracial man—Black and Jewish—he's never fully belonged to one world or the other in the public eye.

He occupies a cultural in-between that people either celebrate or critique, depending on the day. His vulnerability is wrapped in melodies, his emotions delivered through 808s and late-night confessions. And still, despite his massive success, his identity has often been weaponized against him.

There's a line Drake references in his recent music:

"Not Black enough for the Black kids, not Jewish enough for the synagogue."

It's a pain that resonates deeply with me. Being mixed means you're constantly translating, justifying, and explaining. But unlike generations before, who navigated this quietly, Drake has done it all in public.

What makes his experience polarizing is that he's surpassed the expectations often placed on biracial performers—he's not just palatable; he's dominant. And dominance, when you don't check all the traditional boxes, invites scrutiny.

This same kind of cultural gate keeping is happening with artists like Tyla. As her music crosses global boundaries, people online are quick to ask, *"But what is she?"* or *"Is she really Black?"* We've become so obsessed with proving authenticity that we sometimes erase the spectrum of Blackness itself.

In the social media age, everyone has a mic—and a magnifying glass. What's been created is a hyper analysis of racial belonging, where if someone doesn't fit an expected aesthetic or narrative, they're met with suspicion. The focus shifts from the art to the artist's identity—as if it needs to be proven, certified, validated.

But in those debates, we lose the essence of the art—the sound, the message, the emotional connection. We forget that representation isn't about perfection. It's about complexity. Artists like Drake and

Tyla are walking testimonies of how cultural lines blur.

Their existence forces us to ask: Are we truly celebrating diversity, or are we policing it? Is racial belonging based on experience, lineage, or public approval?

In today's world, the line between who we are and how we're perceived is often drawn by algorithms. Identity has become clickable—sorted into hashtags, filtered through comment sections, and broadcast on timelines.

Digital literacy now plays as vital a role in cultural survival as lived experience. Gen Z—with their fluency in tech, timing, and tone—knows how to shape a narrative in seconds. But for those of us who grew up with dial-up and face-to-face conversations, we come from a school of experience that didn't always offer the luxury of rebranding.

I straddle that bridge every day. I've lived the pain of misrepresentation offline, long before it became a trending topic. I've had to explain my presence in rooms, to code-switch before I even knew the word existed. And now I watch a younger generation—both empowered and overwhelmed—carry the digital weight of identity.

They're sharp, socially conscious, and quick to call things out. But sometimes, they lack the patience that comes from living through nuance over time. They can spot injustice in a headline—but may not recognize the silence that comes when no one believes your truth because it wasn't caught on video.

What digital literacy provides in speed, lived experience balances with depth. And that's the bridge I hope to build—not just between generations, but between ways of knowing.

Because representation isn't just about being seen—it's about being understood in a world that rarely stops to ask deeper questions.

Without someone in pop culture who shared my experience, I had to piece my identity together using incomplete parts. I learned to relate to characters who didn't represent me at all. I projected myself into stories that weren't mine, hoping something would stick.

This absence affected more than just confidence. It made me question whether my story was worth telling at all. Because if it mattered, wouldn't someone have already told it?

Pop culture is powerful because it signals who matters. And for a long time, it told me I didn't. So I learned to improvise. To adapt. To mix the Black protagonists I admired with the Asian values I inherited. I became a cultural DJ, remixing bits of what I saw into something I could live with. But even now, I know the difference between seeing yourself and imagining yourself.

I'm still waiting for the day a Blasian character shows up on screen with full humanity—not as comic relief, not as mystery, not as a token or a twist—but as the center.

As someone who looks like me.

And belongs there.

MORE THAN JUST HALF: REWRITING THE FRAME

There was a time when I believed my identity had to be split down the middle.

Half Black. Half Filipino. Half American. Half outsider. I moved through the world trying to portion myself out, like I had to hand over the right percentage to earn belonging in any given space. What I didn't realize back then was that this need to measure myself was rooted in a framework I never agreed to. They weren't built for complexity, for ambiguity, or for those of us who carry entire worlds within.

Maria Root described this space as the "borderland," a landscape of nuance where racial boundaries blur and identities refuse to settle into neat binaries. Her work helped me recognize that the friction I'd always felt wasn't a flaw—it was evidence of authenticity, proof I was fully alive in my complexity.

Yet today, I understand something even Root's wisdom couldn't fully capture: living on the borderland isn't just about surviving between identities; it's about thriving because of them. It's rewriting narratives that once reduced me to "half" and claiming my story as whole, intricate, and inherently valuable.

I spent so much of my life trying to be just enough for everyone else that I forgot how to be whole for myself.

As a millennial with children of my own, I want to pass down more than stories. I want to pass down a framework—a way to navigate the noise, honor complexity, and stay rooted in truth, even when the world tries to edit it.

In a world that moves at the speed of a swipe, I remind myself—and my children—that knowing who you are can't be downloaded. It's learned in layers, through trial and truth, through stories passed down and those we're still brave enough to tell. Our duality isn't a burden—it's a bridge. And across that bridge walks a new generation: curious, clear-eyed, and carrying every note of who we've been into the melody of who we're becoming.

Being racially ambiguous wasn't just an external curiosity for others to poke at. It was a quiet interrogation I carried with me every day. Every glance, every "What are you?", every pause before someone said my name. My presence unsettled assumptions. And over time, I realized that was a gift.

To live between cultures, expectations, and appearances isn't a defect.

It's a lens. I used to look for myself in the world—in classrooms, workplaces, movies, churches, barbershops, and family dinners. And when I couldn't find a match, I wondered if I had done something wrong.

But I hadn't.

The frame was just too narrow. So I'm building a new one. One that sharpens empathy. One that teaches translation. One that holds tension without demanding resolution.

That's what this memoir has been about—not just storytelling, but unlearning. Not just chronicling experiences, but rewriting the frame through which I see them. This story is a blueprint for anyone who's ever felt like they had to downplay their complexity to be understood. For anyone who inherited silence instead of explanation. For anyone whose skin told one story but whose soul carried another. I want my children to grow up knowing that wholeness isn't measured by how well you fit. It's measured by how well you live in your fullness.

I want them to speak freely and cry openly. To claim their lineage without apology. To know that being mixed is not a halfway experience—it's a multilayered one. And that complexity is a strength, not a flaw.

I want them to understand the beauty of duality. That softness and strength can exist together. That tradition and progress are not opposites. That faith and identity can walk side by side.

This journey has taught me that representation begins with self-recognition. That healing starts when we stop translating ourselves for others and start speaking in our natural language. That legacy isn't just about what we leave behind—it's about what we choose to carry forward.

Root opened the door. I've stepped through it, and now, I'm building bridges beyond borders, creating spaces where complexity isn't just tolerated but celebrated.

So if you're reading this and still searching for who you are, let me say this:

You are not too complicated. You are not too mixed. You are not too much. You are more than just half. And the frame was never meant to contain you anyway.

ABOUT

Michael Goodloe is a Black and Filipino storyteller born and raised in Laurel, Maryland—where the intersections of culture, race, and identity shaped the lens through which he sees the world. Navigating life in the DMV as a biracial man taught him early how to move between different spaces, communities, and expectations, often carrying the weight of belonging everywhere and nowhere at once.

His lived experiences—growing up in a multiracial household, confronting racial ambiguity in school and relationships, and learning how to build identity in the borderlands between Black and Asian culture—form the heartbeat of his writing. Michael's work is grounded in honesty, vulnerability, and a desire to give voice to the often-unspoken complexities of mixed-race identity.

Today, he is a father, partner, real estate professional, and advocate for understanding the power and nuance of blended cultures. Through his memoir, *The Blackapino*, he hopes to offer recognition to those who feel unseen in their identities and to inspire readers

MICHAEL GOODLOE

to embrace the fullness of who they are—beyond labels, beyond assumptions, and beyond the boxes society tries to place them in.

Michael currently resides in Maryland with his family. More than a story of mixed race, this is a story of self-reclamation.

For anyone who've ever questioned where they fit or who they're allowed to be—this book is for you.

THE BLACKAPINO

Michelle, Aaron, Miranda, Dominique, Me

MICHAEL GOODLOE

Me on the left, Aaron on the right and Uncle Willy

THE BLACKAPINO

My Dad and I with his military friends at our apartment

MICHAEL GOODLOE

The Filipina wives and girlfriends

THE BLACKAPINO

Me and JK

Google event with Keynote speaker Don Pebbles III

THE BLACKAPINO

Cousin Brother

www.ingramcontent.com/pod-product-compliance
Lightning Source LLC
Chambersburg PA
CBHW030451100526
44580CB00005B/78/J